The BOOK OF BLARNEY

BOOKS OF SIMILAR INTEREST FROM
RANDOM HOUSE VALUE PUBLISHING, INC.:

The BOOK of BLARNEY

ANTHONY BUTLER
Illustrations by Derek Alder

Gramercy Books
New York

This 2000 edition is published by Gramercy Books™, an imprint of
Random House Value Publishing, Inc. 280 Park Avenue, New York, N.Y. 10017 by
arrangement with Wolfe Publishing Ltd.

Gramercy Books™ and design are trademarks
of Random House Value Publishing, Inc.

Random House
New York • Toronto • London • Sydney • Auckland
http://www.randomhouse.com/

Printed and bound in the United States of America.

9 8 7 6 5 4 3 2 1

*To the women in my life, my mother, my wife,
Nora and those exciting, lovely and talented girls,
Denise and Mary.*

Contents

There is a stone that whoever kisses,
O, he never misses to grow eloquent;
'Tis he may clamber to a lady's chamber,
Or become a member of Parliament.
A clever spouter he'll soon turn out, or
An out-and-outer, to be let alone,
Don't hope to hinder him, or to bewilder him,
Sure he's a pilgrim from the Blarney Stone.

The Groves of Blarney.

Blarney Introduction

MUSHA, *Bedad, Begorrah and Bejabers but isn't it we Irish that are the broth of the brewing of God. Oh to be listening to the fine, wandered, wondering weaving of words when we hold the stranger in the heel of our fist and melt his soul and heart in the Irish Stew of the Blarney. And isn't it the wish of the world to be after kissing the Blarney Stone itself and getting the great, gristful gift of words that does be waiting there for all the pilgrims who come to the great castle itself betimes bejabers.*

Oh, isn't it the deep power that does be in words and even long, long ago – and long ago it was – didn't the poets of Ireland slay the enemies of their land: drive rats from granaries and cure the shiverings, the stiffenings and the deluges of the sweat-plague with the sound of their verse.

No doubt there are many people who imagine the Irish express themselves in that fashion although you'd travel far and long before you'd hear one "bejabers" used in normal conversation. On the other hand most visitors to our island are convinced they hear that sort of thing and I have long come to the conclusion that the Irish speech tends to create a Blarney Atmospheric Sonic Warp which gives it a spin so that it is changed completely by the time it reaches the ears of all listeners. On the other hand it seems to change the speech of the Irish themselves back into normal patterns

9

for their own use. Even if the acoustics of Ireland affect our speech patterns it is true to say that Blarney is a real quality and it cannot be ignored or explained away.

What is it?

It's not easy to say what it is and it has been described tamely as an ability to deceive without giving offence – a description that must surely have been thought up by some one who couldn't Blarney. Another said it's the gift of saying the right thing instead of the obvious.

Perhaps it is nothing more than a highly cultivated art of living: the communal radiation of a perfected sixth sense.

Brendan Behan, who was the greatest Blarneyite of all time, could charm the bubbles in porter with scorching abuse no less than if he was treating his victim to shameless praise.

It's words, gesture and atmosphere; it's verbal psychiatry when the subject is stretched on the couch of conversation and environment. One thing – it's no illusion, it's for real. It will seep into the marrow of your bones like a drug and whether we look for love, life or the pounds and dollars falling from your wallet like aged leaves in the gentle breeze of a moon-bronzed Autumn night – it will work.

The Irish Secret Weapon

Blarney is the secret weapon of the Irish. We have enough stockpiled to last beyond the Day of Judgment and we'll dance into Heaven and take no excuse to keep us out. Indeed we are told by the saints of the past that all Irishmen will be judged by St. Patrick on the last day and the country, it is said, will be spared the horrors of Doomsday by a gentle wave inundating it a week before.

As anyone with half an eye can see, the Irish are something special. Let there be no doubt about it – it is established by scientific survey – we are the whitest race in the world.

The lack of pigmentation in our skin is phenomenal. Most of us can't sunbathe a lot as too much exposure of our precious flesh can quickly lead to skin cancer. This again is not guesswork, but a medical fact. One bonus is the unique and flawless complexions of our colleens who are so frequently head-spinning in their loveliness.

We are taller than the European average and if you want a blue-eyed baby – Ireland is the place for you. Almost fifty per cent of the population have this eye-colouring – another of our unique features.

Racially they tell us we come from very ancient Palaeolithic stock with a strong dash of Nordic blood but almost no other European elements. Most of the Irish belong to blood group "O" – another characteristic of pure and ancient people. Take note as well that Irish civilization and culture has a continuous background of five thousand years of history. The civilizations of Greece, Rome and Egypt are mere memories of the past but that of Ireland flourishes unbroken. We don't want to boast but if pressed – well!

The Stone of Eloquence

Blarney, of course, is as old as our race but it is only within comparatively modern times that it got its own shrine in Co. Cork where the Blarney Stone is the great symbol of the peculiar, charming quality of the Irish. It is situated in the Castle of the same name a few miles from Cork city and every year some seventy thousand people climb 120 feet to the dizzy battlements to look for eloquence. At times the medieval winding stair of the Castle is jammed with people going up and down. As they stand on each other's feet, poke cameras in any available eye, dig elbows deep into ribs, it is surprising how eloquent they can become and they speak of each other with a fluency that is admirable even if the choice of language is occasionally deplorable.

The stone itself is a block of limestone about four foot,

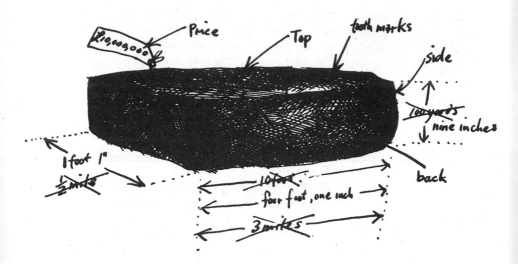

one inch long, one foot, one inch wide and nine inches deep. There is a chip missing in the front, removed it is believed by one of Cromwell's cannon balls when his army besieged the place.

More Precious than Rubies

The value of the stone has been estimated at about ten million pounds and it couldn't be worth more if it was made of solid ruby. The value is calculated on the quite vast sums that have been offered for a brief loan of the thing.

The question of sale or loan is now academic as Sir George Colthurst, who died in 1951, made the Irish Government one of the trustees of the Stone. It is unlikely that any politician would run the risk of annoying the public by allowing the precious relic to leave Ireland even for a short period.

There are several stories about the origin of the stone. It is said that it is Jacob's Pillow brought back from the Holy Land during the Crusades. Some knight packed it in with his spare suit of armour and when his wife was unpacking she asked what it was.

Blarney Abbey, Westminster

Ye ancient knight said, more or less, that if he could get a few more stones like it he might build a castle. It is also said that it is a part of the Stone of Scone or Stone of Destiny which is now incorporated in the Coronation Chair at Westminster. According to this legend, one of the MacCarthys – the Irish family that once owned the Castle – helped Robert Bruce at the Battle of Bannockburn and Robert generously broke off a bit of the Stone of Destiny and gave it as a token of his gratitude. If this is true it means that anyone kissing the stone in the Coronation Chair should also obtain the gift of eloquence – and in that case the edifice should be re-named Blarney Abbey instead of Westminster Abbey.

Another story tells of how Cormac MacCarthy popped into a river and rescued an old lady who handed him as a reward a large hunk of rockery (four foot one inch long, one foot one inch wide and nine inches deep). This it is alleged was the Blarney Stone. We admit to being sceptical. It is doubtful whether even old ladies would go swimming with such a massive hunk of limestone on their person.

Blarneying Good Queen Bess

Queen Elizabeth the First is credited with using the word Blarney in its modern sense. One of her henchmen in Ireland is alleged to have been henching around Blarney trying to persuade one of the owners of the Castle to give up his ancient rights which included quirrens of butter and sroans of oatmeal from his clansmen. The particular MacCarthy involved – no doubt a butter quirren addict and a sroan of oatmeal lover – was slow in making the change.

The *MacCarthy Mor* (the Big MacCarthy) which was his

title, kept putting off the surrender of Cuddy, Sorren, Dowgollo, Rout and Musteroon no less than the quirrens and the sroans. He kept the Queen's henchman at bay and everytime Queen Elizabeth complained there was always a plausible excuse.

The Queen – impatient to grab the Cuddy, the Sorren, the Musteroon and the quirren – screamed in exasperation one day: "Blarney, Blarney – it's all Blarney! What he says he does not mean and what he means he does not say!"

It doesn't really matter and it is the undoubted powers of the Stone that are important. It requires courage to kiss it as the eloquence seeker has to hang down over 120 feet of empty air to get at it. True you get a handsome certificate at the Castle Souvenir Shop but you have to earn it the hard way.

The Word is "Help!"

Even the shyest person will find the gift of words when they try it.

They still speak of the speech I made when, hanging over the awful abyss, I kissed the Stone. Catching a glimpse of the depths below my cry rang out with clear simple eloquence over the Blarney countryside.

"Help! Help! Get me out of here!"

Try it sometime and see what I mean.

Blarneying Back

But whether you go to Blarney or not you'll still be no match for the Irish although we're never too hard on those who come amongst us. Indeed this book is an attempt to give the visitor some advantage because it's shameless to let him in defenceless and unprepared. Not alone will he be able to resist Blarney a little better but he should be able to Blarney right back. In the end, it might as well be repeated, it will make no difference – but at least no one can say we didn't play fair.

We welcome strangers – no place more – and they accept willingly our blatant hypnotism and our narcotic charm. Brainwashed in a million shades of shamrock, they stagger back to the world refreshed in living and with green-laughtered blood going in and out with the tides of Ulster, Leinster, Munster and Connaught. Forevermore their Blarneyed spirit will bear the stamp *Made in Ireland*.

The Blessings of St. Patrick, St. Bridget, St. Kevin, St. Brendan, St. Fursey and the Revolving Indian Saint of Tory Island (see page 133) be on you and yours.

Or to put it another way:

Health and Long Life to you,
Land without rent to you.
A child every year to you.
And if you can't go to Heaven at least may you
die in Ireland.

You are Here

In CASE you get lost in Ireland, it may help to know that the place lies between 51 degrees, 26 minutes to 55 degrees, 21 minutes North latitude and between 5 degrees, 25 minutes to 10 degrees, 30 minutes West longitude.

The average width is about 110 miles and the average length 220 miles. The distance between Ireland and Britain at its narrowest point is only a little over 13 miles, but don't talk about it too much.

Shamrock Sham

ONE HATES to admit it, but the legend of St. Patrick and the shamrock is nothing more than green waffle. He was supposed to have used the plant to illustrate the Christian belief of three persons in one God. There isn't a shred of historical support for this story, but every 17 March we Irish parade with enough of the stuff on our chests to re-create the Hanging Gardens of Babylon.

The chronicles of the past indicate that the Irish ate the stuff rather than wore it. In Elizabethan times an English writer noted, "All the Hibernian kerns in multitudes did feast with shamrags steeped in usquebaugh." They still feast on the whiskey, of course, but minus the shamrags.

The Persians Have a Word for it

It didn't become something of an Irish national symbol until around the seventeenth century. The real shamrock is considered to be the *Trifolium Dubium L.* and it can be distinguished from white clover by its slightly hairy stem and the absence of white markings on the leaves.

What is particularly interesting is the fact that the Persians have a somewhat similar name for a three-leaved plant and they call it *shamrukh.* It too has religious meaning. Looks as if some Irishman Blarneyed his way around the place and left a myth as souvenir of his merry passing. But then, a myth is as good as a smile.

Liquid Paradise

THE BACKBONE of liquid Blarney in Ireland is stout and porter. In countless bars the great pint glasses stand on the counters, each with an attendant worshipper who stares into its ruby-black depths. Others may laugh or gabble but these men just stare and stare. Some of them, it is rumoured, never even drink the stuff.

Irish stout is kindly and soothing; motherly and flattering; gentle and loving. It blesses the digestion like the passing wing of an angel. Beautiful though it is, pride of place belongs to the glory of Irish liqueur whiskey. It is too little known that all Irish pot still whiskey is classified as a liqueur.

By law Irish whiskey must be matured by for at least five years but the great bulk of it is seven years old. Most Scotch whiskies are made by the patent still method which enables large quantities to be produced quickly and cheaply. The Irish pot still process is slower and much more expensive but it locks every last subtle flavour and essence into the drink.

Scowering the Scurf

Irish distillers are not alone in using the pot still method but they give the whiskey three distillings with fantastic results. No wonder Richard Stanhurst wrote of it lyrically in the seventeenth century, ". . . it scowereth all scurf; it sloweth age; it cutteth flegme; it pounceth the stone; it expelleth gavel; it keepeth the head from whirling, the mouth from maffling, the stomach from wambling, the heart from swelling, the belly from wirtching, the guttes from rumbling . . . it is a sovereign liquor."

Wise man, Richard.

Before taking your first glass of Irish whiskey – or renewing your pleasure in the drink – you should fast for three days beforehand. In addition read uplifting books and meditate. On the appointed day have a bath and dress well before heading for the tavern. You should pick a quiet one with a southerly aspect.

Order a double whiskey and don't put water or soda in it. Admire its extraordinary amber depth – a visual distillation of the sun's fingers running through the heavy harvest of the barley. Brace yourself and deeply inhale the odour. It will probe every cell of your lungs with cleansing fingers. It makes the air worth bottling. Then another sip and another – not too fast and not too slow.

Pulse of Bliss

A vast pulse of bliss runs through your body right out to the tip of every delighted hair as it sizzles with alcoholic electricity. A vast host of leprechauns carrying great peat torches moves through your bloodstream.

You close your eyes and you are floating on a carpet of titillating palms which caress you with the gentleness of a lover. You levitate still more.

This state lasts for at least an hour. Although you can drink more – Irish whiskey is noted for the fact that it gives no "morning after" feeling – in circumstances of the kind described it should be one and one only.

Dublin and
Sherwood Forest

AT THE OLD Oxmantown Green in Dublin, Little John of Robin Hood's merry men was supposed to have demonstrated his skill as an archer after the band was broken up. Caught in robbery, the legend has it that he was hanged at Arbour Hill in the city. From the oak woods of Oxmantown the timbers of Westminster Hall were supposed to have come in the days of King William Rufus and it was said of them, "No English spider webbeth or breedeth on them."

Hospitality Blarney

No MATTER who you are, stranger, and no matter where you come from – even that ruffianly town of Lovelock in Pershing County, Nevada – you are entitled to a full ration of *cead mile failte* or one hundred thousand welcomes. Maybe 'tis counting them you'd like to be after doing, but have no fear – it's not the Irish will be stinting you.

You will probably have your first contact with Blarney on your journey into the country. If you've arrived by an Irish-flavoured, friendly airline you will certainly have been processed. On the planes, of course, they call it Bl-AIR-ney and the hostesses will have rinsed your ears with the soft, kind tingling wash of their native accents.

They'll give the rich anaesthetic of an Irish coffee and brainwash or rather Blarney Brain*wish* you into the enjoyment of the trip. This accounts for the fact that most passengers at Dublin Airport step out with their hands stretched before them and their eyes closed. Led by a kindly official they go on repeating over and over again in hypnotised tones, "I am lucky to be in Ireland . . . I am lucky to be in Ireland . . . I am lucky to be in Ireland . . . I am lucky to be in Ireland."

Snapped out of their trance by the patter of the Customs officer – it has been described as the sound of musical plastic hailstones falling on a corrugated rubber roof – they wake to his, "Haveyouanythingtodeclare?–youhaven't?–passalongplease."

Getting to Know Us

From that moment on they are ready to respond to any shamrock-coloured suggestion.

But 'tis not welcome alone that you'll be after seeking, O fine, fair, formidable traveller with your great zoom camera and your telephoto lens slung behind you. You'll be asking to know us and to be slapping our backs with the broad width of your open, generous hand.

But you can be certain of one thing, you won't have to go to too much trouble to know the Irish and it might be wise to avoid knowing them too quickly. We know of one English tourist who offered a cigarette in a friendly way to a native five minutes after he stepped from an Irish airlines plane. Within minutes he was whisked into a gay party and white-skinned, blue-eyed Celts (with or without Nordic blood) were pouring whiskey into him with one hand while borrowing ten pounds until Friday with the other.

Within two hours he came out of his Celtic trance to find himself facing an angry and handsome woman who called him by his first name and told him it was all over between them. Since he had no recollection of the thing starting he was a little bewildered.

She told him she was going out of his life for ever and not even the memories of the past – he still wonders how much "past" you can manage in two hours – would bring her back.

He was last seen in a conscious state around 4 a.m. in the middle of a pack of Dublin citizens all pursuing a rumour that a south-side public house was passing bottles of stout through a street grating in noble defiance of the law. He was found next morning in the hotel laundry, heavily sprinkled with detergent and within seconds of being pushed into the automatic washing machine.

Go in Toe First

This we must grant is an extreme if not totally unusual case but it is wise to treat Irish society like a cold sea at the beginning of May. Test it, metaphorically, with your toe; paddle a little and don't plunge right in until you know the depth, temperature and local currents. A knowledge of the marine life in the vicinity will also help, for Ireland has its quota of odd fish.

In Irish restaurants and bars; in buses and trains or anywhere you choose to go you will find that you are expected to make a lifelong friend in ten minutes. Fortunately the length of a life in circumstances of this kind is usually little more than ten minutes so no harm done.

Ask someone the way back to your hotel and you'll never know where it will end. In a short time you'll have a crowd around you and you won't be able to speak to all of them – you'll have to address them as a public meeting.

At race meetings, football matches, dances or a *Fleadh Ceoil* (Festival of Music) or the special occasions like Puck Fair at Killorglin, Co. Kerry – a pagan fertility festival, where a crowned goat high on a swaying platform dominates the town – you'll be swept into the thing like sand in an hour glass.

Home-brewed Kindness

People will smile at you, shout at you, slap your back, scowl in your eye, praise you, sneer or shake you by the hand like a motor mechanic with a jack handle but one thing – they won't be indifferent to you. In public houses your advice will be sought or you will be lectured on the defects of your own country or have its merits pointed out to you. You'll never lack conversation. It's all part of the Blarney and let it be said Blarney is not the same thing as insincerity. They may deceive you, flatter you and bamboozle you but nine times out of ten it's sheer hospitality and rich home-brewed kindness.

After you've been handed your quota of one hundred thousand welcomes you will be looking for shelter and tables laden with the simmering grandeur of a hundred cooking pots. Indeed to allow the Blarney Atmospheric Sonic Warp to take effect – the high blessing will be yours, stranger, and ye to be touching your toes with your tongue from the sharpening of the appetite on the long, wide strap of the hungering winds of Ireland that do be blowing. 'Tis the fine, fair, full feeding forninst ye, ye'll find, praise to St. Bridget, the holy woman, of the open hand and the patroness of the wide and hospitable gullet.

Indeed hospitality has always been the pride of the Irish. Long ago and long ago it was, there were hostels in ancient Ireland and no one who came the road could be turned away without receiving food and shelter. Strangers were always fed before they were asked their business and everyone had a particular dish in accordance with his rank. For instance a king got a leg of pork, the queen got a haunch and the charioteer got a boar's head which caused a lot of muttering in the charioteers' trade union. They even handed over a wife or two to the guest at the end of the evening and would scarcely take a refusal.

"Think nothing of it," the ancient king would say, "I've got spares."

Wives are Off

It certainly was a good way of Blarneying anyone who came along but the custom is no longer practised. With wives in short supply, you needn't expect to have one handed to you with the dessert. In any event you will be fed well and nowadays there is little fear you will suffer from the ailment mentioned by Giraldus Cambrensis about eight hundred years ago when he wrote of how few visitors to Ireland could hope to escape ". . . a violent flux of the

bowels from the succulent qualities of the food they take."
Today the succulent qualities of the food are even better but
the sturdier bowels of the twentieth century take it in their
stride.

Hotels and guest houses in Ireland – and most Irish
guest houses would be classified as hotels elsewhere – are
strictly graded but the welcome isn't. The visitor is steeped
from the start in a vat of concern and attention.

Mind you there are exceptions, although few and they
don't last long in business. In the *Blarney Magazine* of long
ago it was said that any hotel proprietor who failed to
welcome a guest properly was a man who was quite likely
to sharpen a razor on the tombstone of his father to cut his
mother's throat.

It will be a sad place indeed if they don't press a cup of
tea into your hand on arrival and 'tis solicitous queries will
be made to test your weariness after the journey. Of course

it is also a psychological survey on the part of the hotel to study what technique they will use in giving the Blarney Room-Sell.

Room with a View

Irish hotel rooms are like any others – they come in all shapes and sizes and some are very good and some are less than lovely. With his total desire to make you happy the Irish hotel proprietor will want to Blarney Brainwish you into loving whatever accommodation he offers, for 'tis kindness itself the man or the woman is entirely. If, for instance, you are shown a small, constricted room overlooking the sea, the river or the mountains, the door will be thrown open with a flourish and you will be ushered directly to the window.

"There," says Mine Host proudly, carefully screening the rest of the room from you with his body, "and have you ever then in the whole of your born, natural life ever seen the likes of a view like that? Oh, but isn't it grand and beautiful and the hatchet of Heaven splitting the valleys of the hills and the great skies dropping the milk of beauty into your broad lap."

Depending on the effect he's had he will let you see a little bit more of the room. Like a Pavlovian dog to bells – you must be conditioned to it.

"Sure I said to myself," he'll go on, "when I got your letter and you to be talking about the loveliness of Ireland that you and your wife would have to have the room with the best view in the hotel. Oh, but didn't I sit up the night racking the brain with great combs of thought to pick the one you'd want and I said to myself that Number Six 't'would be and Number Six 'tis."

By the time he's finished both of you will be convinced. Only an unfeeling churl would complain, particularly when he doesn't know that in some other part of the building guests are being shown into a large room with only one window facing a blank wall. There too, the door is thrown open with a flourish and the guide is carefully putting himself between them and the window.

"And now isn't that a fine room I've given to you. Sure when I got your letter I said to myself that you'd see enough scenery during the day and what you'd need at night was a good big cool room for yourself and the Missus."

Only an unfeeling churl would complain particularly when he doesn't know that somewhere else in the building, guests are being shown into a small room without windows. The door there is thrown open with a flourish.

"And now there's a room for you. Didn't I say to myself when I got your letter – now there's a man and a woman that want a nice, small, warm, cosy room and I put this aside for you specially. You'll be as snug here as a bug in a rug."

The Blarney Forward-Fall

The answer to the unsuitable room is the Blarney Forward-Fall. Agree with him that the room is magnificent but point out how unworthy you are of such generosity and kindness. Tell him you want another and since this room is magnificent there'll be no difficulty in getting someone to swap. Don't relent – insist. Most of them will almost collapse from shock at the first attempt to reverse their own techniques.

Don't expect anyone to take much heed of your request for an early morning call in the morning. This is completely ignored in the interest of the guests. It is, the hotel staffs say to each other, a mad and cruel thing to wash the kind feeling of Blarney from the blood of the stranger by bringing him to his senses in the cold, unloving hours of the morning when neither wife, husband nor lover can hear a whisper from their urgent hearts. Oh, no then – the hotel staffs will raise their voices unanimously as they sit at supper – let us not help this man in the wildness of his insanity but

let you and I and she and he protect him and keep him in the warm healthiness of his little roomeen. In other words they let you sleep it out.

Contrary Cocks

This is something a little more than Blarney and the ancient King Cormac Mac Airt put it this way, several hundred years ago; "Worst for the body of the man; sleeping with a leg over the rail of his couch, new beer, gazing at dying embers, dry food, bog water and rising too early." Even the bold Giraldus Cambrensis in 1160 or thereabouts found that cocks crew at different times in Ireland to other countries.

If you want to get up early in Ireland bring your own alarm clock and set it for around 5.30 a.m. You must remember that if the staff catch you at the game you'll be seized and carried back to bed while loud cries will summon doctors, psychiatrists and strait jacket vendors. In your own best interests they can't permit it.

You must not expect to find smooth and mechanical efficiency wherever you go in Ireland. The English with their natural regard for the eccentic find it charming but Americans accustomed to the precision of the drugstore, the "Nite Eatery" and balanced dishes of fried calories with grilled carbohydrate can go slowly mad as they drift around. Mary Toorey, an American girl who fell under the spell of the country and couldn't leave it tells of the experiences of her parents when they came.

Salmon it is, Then

They – and all Americans like them – couldn't grasp that meals in Ireland have their time and place. They wandered into one hotel at six o'clock in the evening and asked, "What do you have for dinner?"

The wee girleen looked at them – bobbed in some friendly way and cried with panic, "I'll be after asking." She fled into some dungeon beyond the dining room and came back with a single word.

"Salmon."

Very well, said the Toorey parents, bring us of your salmon in large and bountiful manner. The girl looked at them with desperate agony.

"But 'tis only teatime now."

The Tooreys looked at each other. The wee girleen unhappy that they should be worried said, "If ye'll wait until half seven you can have the salmon for the dinner."

Mr. Toorey consulted Mary on the ways of the people and they to be feeding the strangers and she gave him whispered instructions.

"O.K.," said Mr. Toorey, "what can we have for tea?"

The wee girleen once more broke down under the executive strain and announced, "I'll be after askin'."

She fled once more. When she came back there was a bright and happy smile on her face.

"Well?"

"Sure there's salmon on the menu for tea."

Black Notebooks are Out

When this sort of thing happens note it in your mind if you are English and write it down if you are American. I would suggest to Americans, however, that they make their notes in private. I have seen strong men flinch when a Long Island tourist produced a huge black notebook and scribbled down her impressions. Big black notebooks in Ireland are associated with the law and questions such as:

"And can ye explain, Flaherty, how fifteen of Mrs. Murphy's chickens are to be found in the fine wide boot of your car?"

No, big black notebooks are to be avoided.

An Irish girleen has been mentioned but although she served at table she could not be considered a waitress. Do not expect Irish waitresses to Blarney you. Serving girleens will do all they can to keep you happy – Irish waitresses will not. No lack of courtesy to you is intended but they have their own troubles and 'tis you will be after trying to bring cheer into their lonely lives. 'Tis said, foreby, that waitresses belong to a monastic order or some kind of a secret society of aged virginity which is in but not of the world. I don't believe a word of it. Irish waitresses are all frustrated women novelists. Watch them. They spend long hours in corners writing in small books; scribbling away their life work. Don't mind the talk of bills and accounts and what bill or account needs the long wide light of the day for its gathering.

"Stay Where Ye Are"

As a result of all this, waitresses in Ireland tend to be remote and aloof. A good solid man from Sheffield – a Sewing Machine Accessories Salesman – told me, with shattered morale, of what happened to him and his family when they went into a small seaside restaurant in Co. Kerry.

He read the menu which was well plotted and had a neat style but which lacked the finer points of Edna O'Brien. No one appeared until he noticed that the waitress was peering at them gloomily through a service hatch like a scientist checking experimental animals in an observation chamber.

When they had all decided on what they would like they made noises indicative of hunger and a need for attention. Tables were rapped and loud coughs rang bronchially through the cosy dining room but nothing happened. To a group accustomed to Blarney attention this was a shock.

They were making preparations to leave when the waitress, who was clearly a Deep Depression if they ever saw one, emerged through a door and said slowly and coldly, "Stay where ye are."

They sank back. It was the Sheffield Sewing Machine Accessory Salesman said, difficult to know what to do. Was it a command, a plea or a warning? Eventually she came to them with the thick bundle of her manuscript in her hand. It was, the Sheffield Sewing Machine Accessory Salesman could see, the Great Definitive Irish Novel.

Almost at once they had her bewildered by a variety of orders. One child wanted sausages, another a mixed salad. His wife wanted an omelette while he himself asked for bacon, egg, sausages and chips. He was, it may be noted, a gourmet.

Cutting the Gordian Knot

Somewhere between his bacon and chips she lost track of the lot and they had to repeat it. They started all over again and this time the waitress like a true novelist gave them all characters. She divided them into the Big Girl, the Little Girl, the Lady and "You". The "You" was of course the salesman himself. It was all explained once more and they were given their parts in the plot as omelettes, sausages, mixed salads and bacon-egg-and-chips.

All seemed well but . . .

In three minutes she was back accusing Mrs. Sheffield Sewing Machine Accessory Salesman of wanting chips with tomato sandwiches. The accusation had to be rejected firmly and even indignantly for one does not want it to get abroad that one is a chips and tomato sandwich woman.

The head of the family decided to resolve the matter and ordered bacon and eggs for everyone. It was, he thought, the cutting of the Gordian knot.

It is impossible to speculate what went on in the mind of the waitress as she contemplated her duty to Irish Blarney and tourism. Whatever it was she emerged some time later with great masses of poached eggs, sardine sandwiches and chicken rissoles. Possibly it was her effort to conciliate them all or it may have been a difficult time with Chapter Seventeen of the Great Irish Novel.

Shakespeare wasn't Irish

No ONE HAS YET claimed with any degree of support that your man Shakespeare was Irish but at the same time the Bard had a touch of green. When Hamlet swears by St. Patrick he gives only one instance of Irish influence on the playwright. Indeed it is worth noting that the original and historic Hamlet was killed by an Irish king.

One of Willie Shakespeare's friends was the Dublin composer and lute player, John Dowland. His influence is to be found in the fact that at least eleven Irish songs are mentioned in the plays.

Anticipating the ballad singers who swarm in almost every Dublin public house twanging guitars like bed springs, the swan of Avon coined a perfect phrase to describe them when he referred to the Irish as "rug-headed kerns". Even today if you spread six or seven ballad singers on the floor you'd find it very comfortable under foot.

The Rheumatic Octopus

Many people still boggle at the thought of "a woolen bagpipe" mentioned in the "Merchant of Venice". It is accepted that this refers to the Uileann Pipes, a native musical instrument that has to be seen to be disbelieved. It looks, one witness has stated, like a rheumatic octopus.

Macbeth is, of course, very Irish and King Duncan, MacBeth and the bloody lady herself are all of Irish descent. The idea of Birnam wood moving to Dunsinane is to be found in an ancient tale of an attack on a Co. Kerry castle by Ulster warriors who disguised themselves as trees.

The three weird sisters have many parallels in Gaelic legend. There is one tale in which three sisters, bewitch the Fianna, the army of the great mythical warrior, Finn Mac Cool. The sisters are described in most versions in a way that can hardly be considered Blarney. They are said to have been oozing and blear-eyed, bandy-legged and rope-haired and they were supposed to have nails on their hands like ox horns. Scarcely the kind of people one would like to mix with socially but blood sisters to the weird ones of "Macbeth".

Irish English

The English of Ireland is a language in its own right and the pronunciation is said by scholars to be similar to that of Shakespeare's day. In Act Two, Scene Five of "Anthony and Cleopatra" you will find the phrases "He is afear'd to come." This usage is still to be heard in rural Ireland. Other examples of our Elizabethan pronunciation are to be found in "speak" which is uttered as "spake"; "cream" as "crame"; "eat" as "ate" and "tea" as "tay"

It has been suggested that Shakespeare visited Ireland at one time. It is probable that Youghal was the place he descended upon but it must be stressed that the support for the idea is not very strong.

Irish Spaceships

ONE OF THE first references to Unidentified Flying Objects is to be found in the eleventh century *Book of Glendalough*. It records that a great ship was seen in the sky at the Tailteann Fair. A spear was thrown from it and a man swam down through the air to take it back. The crowd held the spear until he shouted that he was drowning. The moment he was released he floated back to the space ship which took off into the sky.

A Gloss of Stoat

THERE ARE NOT many unusual or distinct Irish animals, although we are rather proud of our Bull Island mouse which is fairly unique. You can Blarney us about it and your praise will bring a blush to our modest cheek. Above all, however, we take a special pride in the Irish Stoat.

It is well known that the Australian Duck Billed Platypus has no teats with which to suckle its young and one sympathises with both the Australians and the Duck Billed Platypus. On the other hand the Irish Stoat has ten to twelve teats compared with the eight possessed by alien sub-species. Could one say that what has been Australia's loss is Ireland's gain? In any case we feel the Irish Stoat is worthy of the land it lives in.

Gentlemen Please

CLOSING TIME in Irish public houses, particularly outside Dublin, is an elastic thing. One Co. Cork proprietor has a sarcastic notice on his walls which reads: *The Management takes no responsibility for any injuries received in the rush for the door at closing time.*

Once at Lisdoonvarna I was sitting beside an American visitor who couldn't understand why the public house evening wandered on to the following morning.

"Say," he asked his neighbour, "when does this public house shut?"

"Around the middle of next month," answered his neighbour solemnly.

Pub Crawling by Boat

Again in Co. Cork they have a way of avoiding any possible limitation that might be placed on their drinking hours by law. They go on pub crawls by yacht. Along the coast there are several large islands equipped with public houses. Since life is peaceful on the islands no police station is required and supervision of the licensing laws is slack.

Gallant drinkers set sail from Cork and go from island to island and from pub to pub. When the boats go zig-zagging over the seas down there they may not be tacking – they may be plain drunk. On only one known occasion have the drinkers been caught on the islands when they were detected by telescope from the mainland. Even the judge was shocked by such an unsportsmanlike act and he imposed a nominal fine.

Business Blarney

UNTIL THE RECENT past Ireland was a happy country where the absence of snakes was reinforced by a complete ignorance of such things as a Balance of Payments, a Gross National Product or an Import-Export problem. A happy land, as you might guess. Then someone thought it was internationally odd that we shouldn't have the same set-up as everyone else and in no time we were knee deep in prosperity – which declare to Heaven no one could afford. No use now lamenting the glorious days when we lived in merry poverty and bankrupt contentment.

It must be admitted that we've taken to the export business in great style and we send souvenirs to Hong Kong; mountains of milk powder to South America and a vast assortment of other items to quite unimaginable places. On one memorable occasion a camel train was reported on the road to Jericho laden with packs all stamped "Candles – Made in Ireland". This is perfectly true but as yet no one has dared ask how this order was obtained. Nor can one guess why Bedouins – or even Double-Bedouins – should so desperately need our candles.

The Blarney

It is no surprise, of course, that the Irish are good at creating exports. In their home areas they have always

been among the world's best businessmen and the Blarney Sell is irresistible. Most people coming to Ireland will meet it in our shops and then some.

At the height of summer it is a pleasant thing to wander through the larger Dublin stores and listen to the sweet cash register chimes ringing out over the meadows of merchandise. In the background there is a faint metallic whisper as countless American, British, German, Italian, Saudi-

Arabian, Japanese and Australian visitors write out cheques.

Most of this is voluntary and one rarely comes across a South African diamond mine owner or a New York real estate speculator being forcibly held down on a counter by six stalwart assistants while a determined store owner rifles his pockets. This hard sell is to be deplored as it could give the country a bad name, but there are circumstances in which it is justified. If you happen to be a South African diamond mine owner or a New York real estate speculator you can expect no less if you spend half an hour in our shops without buying anything. Patience and good will have their limits.

In their more relaxed moments, of course, Irish store owners lament that the ideal stage has not yet been reached. This will come when a reasonable quota of American millionaires, Arabian sheikhs, German industrialists and other members of the world's wealthy set are compelled to attend with the staff at 9 a.m. each morning to put in a solid eight hours buying. If, as one shopkeeper has stated with solid logic, the staff have to put in a full day, why shouldn't the wealthy customers do the same?

Ink – and the Rest

The whole basis of the Blarney Sell is the deep interest every one has in your welfare. They are not trying to sell you goods – they are trying to satisfy your needs. Take for instance the case of the London stockbroker who went in to a Dublin store and asked for a bottle of ink.

"Is it ink you'll be needing? 'Tis a sad thing and a cruel thing surely and you to be wanting to write home to your family and tell them of the grand things you've seen and the ways it is that you are enjoying yourself in the green, healthy air of the country and not the black scrapings of an inkpot to be on you."

The sweet, wee stockbroker innocent of the customs of

the land was a little bewildered to find his simple request transformed into a major crisis in his life. With a stock-brokerish blush he accepted the comforting sympathy.

"But 'tis a pen you'll want to go with the fine ink I'll be selling you; a pen full of the great, soft words of blessing; a pen that will dance with learning across the fine paper you'll buy with it and you to be resting your weary arms on the lovely, antique mahogany desk you'd be foolish not to take as well. . . ."

An hour later a bewildered and dazzled little London stockbroker was surveying a bottle of ink, six fountain pens, three reams of best-quality linen notepaper with his family crest; a Waterford cut-glass inkstand; a gold desk calendar; a gross of paper clip packages; five hundred hand-embroidered Irish linen pen wipers; a stone of blotting paper and a silver-mounted Connemara marble paper knife.

As the shop assistant put it, "And wouldn't the ink now be a useless thing without the rest."

He was perfectly sincere and if he was a Boy Scout, he would feel happy that his day's quota of good deeds had been over-produced.

All Things for All Men

It is this intimate bond between you and the shopkeeper that makes Irish shopping so interesting and refreshing. The concern is even greater in Western areas where they run what must be the prototype of the departmental store. Somewhere beyond the bicycle repair section you'll see a bar merrily dispensing drink amid the overflow of the drapery department. There is little that one man needs that can't be supplied. In such places a well-tied gag is essential.

Passing one of them in Donegal, a Yorkshire Nylon Yarn Spinner, already financially dehydrated in shopping encounters, warily greeted the shopkeeper at the door with the elementary and apparently safe remark that it was a very hot day. The proprietor leaped eagerly to be of service.

"Is that so then? Well maybe it is yourself that would like to be buying an electric fan?"

"No, no," cried the Y.N.Y.S. with fear. "It wouldn't be of any use. I haven't got a power supply to carry around."

"Never say die," the shopkeeper exhorted, raising a comforting hand. "I can sell you a portable generator and all you need is a wheelbarrow – and I stock the best – to push it about and work the fan. 'Tis the height of comfort ye'll have. Wait, I'll get them."

"No, no, no," shrieked the Y.N.Y.S. "I'll cool off some other way."

"A whipped cream ice cone ye'll be. . . ."

"I'm going in for a swim in ten minutes. Thanks, thanks, thanks."

The shopkeeper had not exhausted his resources or his eagerness to serve.

"Swim suit? Water wings? Maybe 'tis Your Honour might like to hire a boat and go for a swim in the middle of the Bay? Now I can. . . ."

"I have to go down to the beach. I've got to hurry, I must. . . ."

"You'll need to hire a car so and I'll call my son Francie to . . ."

Finally the Y.N.Y.S. took the situation into his hands and dashed.

"Got to fly," he giggled nervously, "can't let the grass grow under my feet, you know. . . ."

He was gone but on the breeze the words wafted to his ears.

"An airline reservation? A lawnmower. . . . ?"

Substitutes Without Tears

It can be taken that it all springs from consideration and a desire to please. This can take many forms and if the shopkeeper hasn't got what you want – horror of horrors! He will not waste time lamenting but without the slightest delay will seek a substitute.

One man in from the hills looking for a television set in his local hardware shop – which didn't sell them – was persuaded to invest his money in a large-scale compendium of games instead. Bewildered he took it away and when last seen he was desperately trying to bring in a good signal from Welsh television on the ludo board. Exceptional, perhaps, but a good example of what can happen.

Another visitor tells of the narrow escape he had in Co. Waterford when, going abroad without a coat, he found himself sheltering in the doorway of a small draper's shop while in the street the rain tore up the road like multiple pneumatic drills. The draper stepped out beside him.

"Soft day," he said.

"Misty," said the visitor as the gutters overflowed and sent them into the shop before the order was issued to abandon ship. Then it occurred to him that a draper's shop was a good place to buy a plastic raincoat.

The draper winced when the request was made.

"Ochone," he groaned, "there isn't one in the town."

Then he brightened.

"Rubber boots?" he suggested hopefully.

"No thanks."

He corrugated his brow and then his face lit up like a 200-watt bulb.

"I have the thing for you," he chuckled triumphantly, "'Tis you will be as snug as a bug in a rug in this."

He vanished into the back of his shop while the visitor considered the conviction of the Irish that bugs in rugs have it laid on with hot and cold in every thread. Obviously no judgment should be made until the views of the bug are properly canvassed.

The draper returned with a stack of plastic tablecloths.

"Try one," he urged, "and in your born days you'll never find a better rain cape than that which I'm showin' to you now. Heaven bless us and save us."

Superficially it seemed a very good idea and the visitor allowed a particularly ghastly specimen covered with golden

harps and abscess-green round towers to be draped around
his shoulders. It was fearful but it would keep out the rain.
The pattern, however, made it impossible. He asked for
more.

The supply was limitless but the general appearance was
awful. The rain, with Blarney salesmanship, was still beating
against the window. He might have taken one with a printed
firelit interior and the happy slogan in ten inch letters,
"Home, Sweet Home", if the shopkeeper with an unwise
burst of zeal hadn't wrapped it around his head and pinched
it under his chin. It was too much: he looked like a plastic
leprechaun. The would-be customer took one look and then
fled into the downpour without lifebelt or boat.

Sincere Deception

Good-humoured, pleasant and deeply interested in
people, the Irish make top-quality businessmen and their
Blarney is a wonderful asset. Even when they are putting

one over on you they are absolutely sincere in their deception. It works wonders.

If you want to try the Irish technique you should bear in mind (Bedad!) that you must not aim to sell goods and services – you should first try to sell yourself. It is this highly personal element that explains Business Blarney.

Time and time again American and English sales managers and vice-presidents have descended on us to show their native employees how to do the job. They set up courses for the salesmen and drill them in the key points of the product, the hard sell, the psychology of the customer, and think they are set to sweep the country. They even go around with the salesman to see how it goes. Alas for their hopes – they are usually disappointed.

The Irish shopkeeper doesn't want technical details but he does like the salesman to ask after the children, to enquire about the health of the family and to tell him the latest bit of gossip from the last customer. When he's got all this and if the salesman has impressed him he looks at the product.

The sales managers and the vice-presidents go slowly mad and stick shamrock in their hair as planned selling techniques perish in a soft flood of Blarney. As they desperately try to stem the tide they find themselves buying sticks of candy, rubber boots, dried fish, lottery tickets and a host of items offered. There is one shopkeeper in Limerick who boasts he couldn't live if he didn't sell so much to visiting sales managers.

How's the Wife, the Wife, the Wife . . . ?

What's more, the Blarney Sell can be worked in any part of the world and it can be imagined that the order for candles from Jericho was obtained by an Irishman who asked after the sheikh's health, enquired after all the wives and patted all the forty-eight children of the family on the head. No doubt the candles were slipped into the conversa-

tion as an afterthought, leaving the sheikh to ponder later on what in the name of Allah possessed him to order a fifty-five-year supply of the things.

The introduction of modern economics to the Emerald Isle did at least give it a fresh vocabulary injection. Irish executives love to rattle off the terms of management theory and practice, as if they were something out of the works of Willie Yeats, the poet. They toss them back and forth in conversational ping pong and it's a joy to hear.

PISC, PLPF and DQTHCP

"My dear Murphy (Bejapers!) our Predetermined Inventory Stock Control – or if you wish our PISC – is, smoothwise, working. Once we co-ordinate all the productivity factors of our Parallel Linear Programme Flow (Musha!) we should . . ."

"Interesting you should say that, Kennedy, as I meant to tell you about our Critical Path Analytical (Yerrah!)

Network Technique which gives us (Musha!) a strategic quantification of discrete decision elements . . ."

"Before you go further, Murphy, let me recommend that you consider harnessing the Decimal Queuing Theory Harmonisation of Capital Projections – otherwise DQTHCP – to your method . . ."

This goes on and on and you need a notebook to keep up with PISC, PLPF or DQTHCP. Bring an Irish executive a new piece of business jargon and you have Blarneyed him into lifelong friendship. In fact he'll dash out to meet you anytime if you give him a chance to discuss USELESS (Unintelligible Statements Entailing Lashings of Endless Semantic Slop). You can make an appointment for the meeting if you wish but always bear in mind that meetings in Ireland are all expressed and arranged in Blarney Time.

Blarney Time

"When God made time," say the Irish, "he made plenty of it." It's something they never forget. They will teach you how to be efficiently unpunctual and what's more you'll enjoy it. Blarney timekeeping is most relaxing and it can give you a holiday during business hours.

It is widely accepted that an Irish or Blarney appointment is elastic. While you will meet people who believe in being on time they are heretics to decent, graceful Blarney living.

Not that the Irish are really unpunctual, they have a peculiar internal time mechanism that keeps them an hour or two behind the clocks. If you translate two o'clock as three o'clock you'll find that there is an upside down form of Blarney punctuality in existence.

One of the things that makes this sort of practice acceptable is the habit in Ireland of arranging all appointments for restaurants, pubs and coffee shops. Half the refreshment trade of the country is generated by people waiting for other people. Not alone does this make unpunctuality tolerable – in many cases it makes it absolutely delightful.

In spite of all this don't get the idea that the Irish are lax in business. Far from it. When they extract your back teeth you can be sure the next effort will be to sell you a dental plate. Remember those candles in Arabia.

The Fleadh Cheoil

FLEADH CHEOIL is the Irish word for a feast of music but the thing itself is much more than that. Every year it is held in a different town and thousands of traditional musicians arrive for three days of intoxicated wonder.

The formal competitions are the official reasons for the thing but the reality is to bathe a whole area in singing, dancing and the playing of musical instruments. In public houses, shops, hotels, and more often or not in the streets, little groups of musicians gather surrounded by crowds and they play on until exhaustion makes them stop. Drink flows everywhere and there is a fairy-like quality in the magic happiness that cuts off one town from time or place for a few days.

There is nothing like it in the whole wide world and there never will be. Here the old Gaelic songs are sung, holding in their heart the melancholy and dignity of five thousand years; somewhere else a wild jig sets feet tapping and heads spinning with the time-polished impact.

Three days it lasts, but sure it takes a week to get the last of the musicians away and they linger on for longer in some cases. *Fleadh Cheoils* do not die – they only fade away.

The Black Irish

MONTSERRAT is one of the Leeward Isles in the West Indies. It is predominently Negro but among its six per cent who are of mixed race or coloured are those who are proud to call themselves the Black Irish.

The island itself is called the Emerald Isle of the Caribbean and it has many historical and sentimental links with Ireland. Government House, for instance, is decorated with shamrocks and the crest of the island shows the usual allegory of Ireland as a woman holding a harp.

Many Irish landowners and peasants were shipped to the West Indies by Oliver Cromwell and many others went as businessmen and traders. From these the Black Irish derive their link with Ireland. Indeed, Anthony Gwynn has called Montserrat the most distinctively Irish settlement there.

Gaelic Twist

Today the estates on the island have Irish names and many families use the word "Irish" as their surname. But there are other manifestations of Celtic origin.

The English used on the island has a distinct Gaelic twist in some cases. The islanders are very likely to say, "I do be closing the door" instead of "I close the door." Dances of the people are closely akin to Irish set dances and the tambourines used are very similar to the goatskin *bowrans* of Co. Kerry. These too are played with the back of the hand in the manner of Irish traditional musicians.

What is more the Black Irish have an easy way of talking that has been described as Blarney. With a true Celtic instinct they are willing to talk about the weather or their health at the drop of a hat.

This strange outpost of Ireland has been studied by John C. Messenger and his wife while working for the Folklore Institute of Indiana University and they have published several accounts of their investigations. Montserrat proved what was once said – that wherever there are people you'll always find an Irishman.

Sex Blarney

IN IRELAND it is well to remember that sex is an eight letter word spelt M-A-R-R-I-A-G-E. Reading about their white skin – the whitest in the world – and calculating that there must be about three thousand acres of the stuff covering some of the shapeliest underlying bone structures in Europe, the male visitor may be inclined to rub his hands and drool at the mouth with lust. He should undrool and de-lust himself. All anticipation is vain.

It's got to be faced that Irish women are truly virtuous and chaste. Blarney may do a lot with them but beyond a certain point the Irish maiden has limitations which can be described as No Man's Land. Nothing has changed very much since Frank Harris wrote of his absolute failure with a girl in Ballinasloe and finished with his irritated complaint, "How do the Irish come to have this insane belief in the necessity and virtue of chastity?"

Frank should have known because he was himself Irish and had experience of women – or so he said – all over the world.

The Six Gifts

Even President "Teddy" Roosevelt got in on the act and in an article in the *Century Magazine* of January, 1907, he laid down the law for Irish girls and more or less said that

their six great gifts should be, ". . . beauty, soft voice, sweet speech, wisdom, needlework and chastity." More American interference with the rights of free nations!

There may be a few exceptions who help to give a different impression, but an old Irish proverb invented recently says, "One road will suffice for ten thousand chariots."

It might be wondered why Sex Blarney should be so ineffective but it is easier to understand when it is appreciated that most Irishmen – including myself – have doubts about the existence of women. This applies even to married men.

We've read books and we've seen pictures but the thought can't be avoided that they may be faked. Even the glimpses we may catch of native torsos at the seaside are not altogether convincing, for no one on the island has ever really seen a woman.

Of course we have to accept that a group goes around calling itself women but they've never really established that they are distinctly different. For instance, all Irish married women have developed an undressing technique which maintains the mystery. They retire into voluminous nighties like Arabs into a tent and toss their clothes out through the neck. When dressing they merely reverse the process and drag in what they want until finally they emerge almost completely dressed. Husbands just sit around and guess.

Irish Women DO Exist

Personally I've come around to the view – although I have yet to convince my wife – that it is distinctly possible that women exist. Much of what follows is written on that assumption, even though I may be sticking my neck out.

One reason for the cold attitude of the Irish female is whispered to be their belief that because they eat a goodly number of potatoes they are very fertile and so daren't take risks. This is nonsense and we have the word of Redcliffe N. Salaman, F.R.S., in his great work *The Influence of the Potato on the Course of Irish History.*

He states emphatically – and Redcliffe N. Salaman is not to be treated lightly – that, "There is nothing in the potato which excites concupiscence or encourages pregnancy." The same reason was advanced for the chill attitude of Scottish girls but here again the kilt swingers stayed off the spud because it wasn't mentioned in the Bible. Your ancient Scot was finicky.

Irishmen haven't bothered to Blarney their own girls properly and you'll often hear them utter the pious prayer, "From thorny bushes, barbed wire and women, Sweet Saints of Heaven, protect me." Not that it was always so and an old Irish king put it on record that the best three things in life were ". . . a song of victory, a praise well earned and an invitation to a lady's bed."

Going Through the Mill

On the other hand, the saints of Ireland made things
tough for the man with the roving eye. St. Fechin had a
mill at Fore in Co. Meath and he made a rule that no
women should enter it. The Normans around 1172 or so
were marching by when one of the army reached out and
grabbed a local peasant girl and taking her into the mill he,
as the historian puts it, ". . . had his way with her." But he
wasn't getting away with it and he "was struck with infernal

fire in the offending parts. It spread through his whole body and he died that night."

Rugged, one must admit, and a warning to the philanderer in Ireland to check on local curses before putting a mill to improper use.

One of the things that has contributed to the idea that women do not exist in Ireland is the fact that when they were first discovered no one knew what to do with them.

"Interesting," one can imagine one ancient Celt saying to another ancient Celt, "but I do not hold (Bejapers!) with these new-fangled inventions. Now that we're stuck with it, what can we use it for?"

Anyone Got Change for a Cumal?

Someone pointed out that there was a shortage of small change and, believe it or not, they used them as money. It is a fact that in Ireland long ago women did go from hand to hand exactly like a silver dollar. They were called cumals. Anyone buying a chariot or a black bull would put down his deposit of ten cumals or women and guaranteed the remainder at two each week. What they did when they had to break a fiver is not recorded.

Take all this into account and no one can blame the modern Irish girl if she is a little frigid and takes for her motto the slogan of the French army before Paris in 1914: *They Shall Not Pass*. Not that this explains everything.

The truth is that all Irish women have the instincts of some species of spider. The man, they plainly indicate is only a stepping stone on the road to motherhood and that's the Irishwoman's true vocation.

What remains is a question which the clean-limbed, purehearted, handsome male must ask himself as he stands on the green shores of the Emerald Isle. Am I then to be deprived of the love-Blarney of the fair, blue-eyed women of Ireland? Am I not to whisper the beguiling words of a stranger into their deep, resonant, white ears?

The answer is a definite, "Most certainly not." Once the alien male accepts the restrictions he will find that access to the three thousand acres of white Irish female flesh – not to mention the underlying bone structure – is not completely barred.

Mini-Blarney

It is a fact that many Irish girls can be Blarneyed to yield a little if you get them alone in a very small car. It is a peculiar thing and it can't be hereditary since those cars are not around that long.

The slick visitor then, who is wishing to be after heading for Blarney romance must be sure to equip himself with the essentials – a mini car and no less important, an Irish girl. There are preliminaries, of course.

There will have to be a few meetings, but the main thing is to get her to accept an invitation to a meal. This is the real test and it is a fact that the true-blooded Irish girl tends to become romantic on steak (medium rare) and crisp French-fried potatoes. Don't ask why – just note it down as a major romantic weapon and a fairly clear guide to the hormone level in the bloodstream of the woman.

Don't rely on your experience outside Ireland where wine, gin or champagne does the trick for the international Romeo. Wine only makes the Irish girl giggle – and giggles are fatal to romance. You can have the girl on a mountain side; you can be babbling about the moon (with, if possible, a reference to June); your heart; her beauty and anything else you can think of but the moment you reach out to fold her into your arms, like an egg into a cake mixture, the alcohol takes effect. What, dear friend, can you do with a woman who gurgles with long rippling giggles. Nothing – and you might as well face it. It is the moment for a clean-limbed, pure-hearted handsome male to cut his losses.

The Unseductive Omelette

This is not to say that a little wine to a vast quantity of steak and French fried potatoes is useless. It can throw a little fuel on the flames of interest. But bear in mind that it is the steak, the whole steak and nothing but the steak that matters. Having got the girl into a restaurant, you hand her

the menu and wait with tense anxiety. This is the moment of truth . . . but don't force the pace.

If she orders an omelette, you've had it and all plans for seduction might as well be abandoned. An omelette-stuffed girl has no zest or interest in sex and it is not the night. Chops and grilled tomatoes are interesting but unreliable; it may be the green light but you can't depend on it. Fish is a definite warning. You'll get warm intellectual conversation on Soul and the future of liberalism in modern society but no more.

If, however, she runs down the menu and after shy hesitation – what woman likes to reveal her heart too quickly? – selects a *Grilled Steak A La Bordelaise* or an *Entrecote A La Mirabeau*, you are knee-deep in four-leaf clover. A delicately grilled and well-flavoured sign has been given that some – the more public areas at least – of that pure white skin and the underlying bone structure are almost within your grasp.

Some indication of the sex-calorie content of various dishes is useful and the following is a good rough guide to the hormone level of any girl who selects them.

Blarney Sex-Calorie Counter

Eggs (Boiled, Fried, Poached)	***Zero.*** *Arctic frigidity.*
Plaice and Chips	*1. Siberian temperature emotionally.*
Drisheen (see page 150)	***Absolute Zero.*** *Subject kicks companion over left eyebrow and gallops into the night.*
Grilled Salmon Steak	*3. Subject will allow hand-holding but she becomes ticklish if she takes a mixed salad with it.*
Matelote A La Bourguignon	*5. Warmer. Subject will listen to blue jokes and permits biting of right ear lobe.*

Meat Balls in Tomato Sauce	**6.** *Can be promising but subject tends to become sentimental and may waste valuable time talking about her old Irish mother.*
Irish Stew	**6.** *Useful but suffers from the same defect as the Meat Balls. Subject tends to be patriotic and violently condemns the Base, Brutal and Bloody Saxon.*
Chicken in Champagne Oasis	**7.** *Subject permits ear nibbling; light kissing and handling of underlying bone structure. Can be socialistic so see she doesn't get the left wing.*
Grilled Chop and Chips	**10.** *Progress. Will tell blue jokes and later will allow a modest ration of after-meal mini-car-caresses.*
Grilled Steak	**20.** *Victory. The subject tends to pant and if bitten on the right ear lobe is liable to bite right back. Permits embraces that her mother would approve of. Her mother isn't around so be satisfied with what you've got.*

Love Among the Cromlechs

Do not attempt any form of personal Blarney during the meal – the Celtic maiden likes to bring an undisturbed knife and fork to the thing and abhors excess conversation with it. Mutter gently, if you wish, about your desire to look on an ancient Irish megalithic tomb or a cromlech by moonlight. The suggestion will get through and when the Celtic maiden has almost scoffed her *Strawberry Flan Chantilly* – for woman does not live by steak alone – she will be eager to show you one. The Irish countryside is littered with such ancient monuments and the Megalithic-Moonlit-Tomb-Blarney can be employed almost anywhere in the land.

At this point introduce the mini car with an air of look-what-I-had-all-the-time-and-never-knew-it. Stuffed with steak protein the Celtic maiden with many a girlish shriek will leap for it like a Galway Blazer over a stone wall.

"Let ye be after then starting yer motor," she'll communicate through the Blarney Atmospheric Sonic Warp, "and I'll bring ye to a fine megalithic tomb that will warm the blood of your heart into wild jigs and shamrock-frilled joy."

The 20th-Century Chastity Belt

You reach for your clutch – if she has no objection – and away. It may, however, before you start, be of value to know what the latest research and surveys have dredged up on the Celtic maiden and the mini-car. The basic advantage of the small car was expressed accurately by one female.

"Nothing serious," she said, "can happen to Irish womanhood so long as it stays put in the front seat. The chaste kiss and respectful embrace are all made for the smaller automobile, but if he forgets himself he's had it. Any attempt at more advanced loving will result in the Celtic or visiting male breaking his head off the roof or splintering his shin on the hand brake. It just isn't possible. In more eager moments he could fracture his spine off the rear window parcel shelf."

"Heaven," added a shrewd Cork colleen, "may protect the working girl but it never did the job half as well as the mini-car."

A more sophisticated woman junior lecturer puts it yet another way. "The small car is the chastity belt of the twentieth century."

Where Were We?

Meanwhile back to the starting pit . . .

You have now got yourself, one assumes, all that the situation requires, namely: one Celtic maiden stuffed to the gills with steak and French fried; one megalithic tomb or round tower; one moon; one mountain; some trees; a ration of whispering winds and, if possible, the soft fragrance of a fern-graced night. Mini-movement One consists of a *glissando* and *pianissimo* movement of the arm along the back of the seat.

The Blarney technique in this situation is simplicity itself. Conduct the conversation on the highest level and don't pretend that there is the slightest connection between what you say and what you do. Speak about round towers – but avoiding Freud at all costs – and tell of your admiration for Ireland of the fourth and fifth century. If you can get the colleen to give you a brief history of Irish tomb builders it should be possible to close your hand over her shoulder without protest.

One American student is reputed to have reached quite an advanced stage of embrace by encouraging the girl to express her opinion of the influence of Irish missionary saints on European culture. She had gone over the arrival of St. Fursey in France in 644 A.D. and told of his disciple St. Gobain whose relics are still honoured in the French town of the same name.

She was speaking with approval of St. Dymphna of Geel

and the Irish Benedictine Schottenkloster at Nurnberg in Germany when she realized that more than his attention had begun to wander. A prudent discretion forbids detail but we must record that virtue triumphed.

St. Ita and the Stag Beetle

It is, of course, a matter of speculation what might have happened if she had been involved in a detailed description of the passage graves at Knowth which take about three hours to outline. One can only speculate that the spirit of St. Ita the foster mother of St. Brendan the Navigator may have hovered over the girl. St. Ita knew what it was to be tempted and she kept a great stag beetle on her body to chasten herself and complained in a poem of the unwanted attentions of ill-minded monks. She should find a place beside St. Christopher in the Irish mini-car.

The clean-limbed, pure-hearted handsome male visitor who has managed to get an Irish colleen to a mountain side will not as the Norman soldier did in the mill at Fore "have his way with her". But there is no reason why he should not take away some happy memories of his experience if he accepts that she will not – in the language of Victorian novels – Yield her All to him. Her All is reserved for more permanent arrangements.

Since it isn't difficult to mix socially in Ireland a girl visiting the place will have no difficulty in contacting the men. What dangers does she face from Blarney?

The Romantic Sprinter

A good many, it must be admitted. While the Irishman has no stomach for the marathon of marriage he is one of the world's greatest romantic sprinters. In the hundred yard dash of the quick and torrid affair, he has no competition if given a clear field. This may suit the girl visitor who wishes to do no more than taste the quality of the Irish.

If Irishmen doubt that the native woman exists they have no such inhibitions about the foreign, American or English female. These, he is convinced, are all confirmed nymphomaniacs. He has been taught from an early age that the world outside is Depraved by the easy morals of a Society that has Abandoned Traditional Virtues and Yielded Itself to Its Animal Instincts. Thank Heaven for it, mutters the Irish male, as he reaches for the alien women, and where would he be at all, at all, were it not for that.

He gets a shock to discover perhaps, that women are women are women are women. He will sulk when he discovers they scorn his mini-car and mock his differential-geared, traverse-sprung chariot of love. He recovers quickly, however, and accepts good-humouredly that the female alien's All is not given automatically. At this point he switches on the Love Blarney and Atmospheric Sonic Warp. In no time he'll be embroidering a tapestry of verbal threads to cloak the daring physical advances he's making. Even at long distance he can be hazardous. There is one instance of an Irish lover being so beguiling with his pen that he brought a Spanish colleen from Madrid to Dublin and she ready to lay down her mantilla for him and he, foolish nut, thinking it was something else.

The Survivor's Version

One American girl who survived the ordeal and came back to tell has reported that what most impressed her – apart from an uncanny technical skill with buttons, zips and eye-hooks – was the flow of words which to her sounded like this:

"*Oh, but isn't it you, agradh, that has the black, shining hair like to the glittering wings of ravens that do be flying in the broken, sad loneliness of the castles of Eireann. Isn't it you that stands as straight as a saintly round tower or Finn Mc Cool's great spear itself. Ah, 'tis singing I would be of your bright, proud skin dazzling the day and breaking the night with the great flashing of its beauty and 'tis the like of you surely was Deirdre and the lovely women of the Gael. Fine, fine is your body and the great moons of your bosom to be lighting the torches of the blood . . ."*

I gathered that her own conversational contributions were simple and might be listed as follows:

"Here . . ."
"What do you think you're . . . ?"
"Now, look, if you . . ."
"I've told you already . . ."

Not very brilliant perhaps, but what can one expect from American girls? In the end, of course, she was murmuring with bliss, "Oh, darling Patrick Emmanuel Pascal . . ."

The Pash Dash

The Irish lover is lazy and he has the instincts of a harem master. A man, he believes, should be loved and he will try to Blarney the woman into the active part. Don't give in, and he'll eventually accept the dominating role. The Irish "pash" dash is, however, recommended to the discerning female alien.

Optimists sometimes come to Ireland and imagine they will seduce some innocent little Celtic housewife with the twang of their Brooklyn or Mid-West accent and even a few pilgrims from Piccadilly Circus have had the same idea. Alas, for the dreamers, they have no hope. Irish wives, in general, have no interest in sex and it is their normal view that the habit is largely the concern of the unmarried.

"Why," said one of them to me once, "should I bother about a thing like that? Sure amn't I married."

The Irish wife is, nonetheless, an absolutely charming person and she'll honestly Blarney you into an admiration for her cheerful personality and her ripe maturity. She'll go with you to see megalithic tombs by moonlight but all you'll do is see megalithic tombs by moonlight. There is one thing to be said for her – she is the world's finest mother. The cute, far-seeing baby will not alone weigh the advantages of dying in Ireland; he will also arrange to be born there. Irish wives are kind, sympathetic, understanding and soothing and if you are in trouble they are a psychological poultice for the weary spirit. One cannot have enough of them.

A Holiday from Sex

In a nutshell, it can be said that for the majority of male visitors to Ireland the best approach is to treat the visit as a holiday from sex. It can be very bracing and refreshing and you too may find as you leave that you are cherishing doubts about the existence of Irish women as a sex. And so the Blessing of St. Ita and her stag beetle be upon you and your mini-car. . . .

Bottles Long Ago

LORD CHESTERFIELD (1694–1773) was Lord Lieutenant of Ireland for a time. He did much for the country but he once said, ruefully, "I wish every man in Ireland were obliged to make as many bottles as he empties, and your manufacture would be a flourishing one indeed."

That's a toast that any Irishman could use as an excuse for another drink.

Ghosts and Leprechauns

THE BEST SPIRITS in Ireland are bottled but there are a few haunted houses and castles to be found. A good account of many of them is to be found in Hans Holzer's *The Lively Ghosts of Ireland* (Wolfe Publishing Ltd., 6s., Hardbound 25s.) Leprechauns are no longer so plentiful as they were and can only be seen at the witching hour of half past two bottles of Irish whiskey. They are remembered and treated with respect just the same, and horror and curses still await the man who would touch a "fairy fort". One of these earth rings lay across the planned path of a Shannon Airport runway. It didn't go.

No workman could be found to shift it and the runway was re-planned. And quite right too!

World's Greatest Liar

ABOUT TWO and a half miles south of Killarney in the quiet churchyard of Killegy lies the grave of Rudolf Ehrich Raspe (1737–1794) who as the writer of *The Travels and Adventures of Baron Munchausen* has a permanent place in world literature. Rudolf Ehrich was quite a character himself.

Something of a scientist, he was employed by the landgrave of Hesse as Keeper of Gems. Rudolf Ehrich got the idea – he kept them. Fleeing to England he worked for Sir John Sinclair and his book on Munchausen, the fantastic liar, was published in London.

He came to Killarney in 1793 to work as geological adviser to the Herberts who were developing lodes at Muckross. Raspe died at Killarney, so when you read of Munchausen you should remember that he now has a Blarney flavour.

Blarney drinks

IT IS WIDELY held that you can't make a real Mint Julep without Irish whiskey. You need one teaspoonful of sugar, a dash of Irish soda water (it was invented in Ireland) or

water; three or four sprigs of mint and a wineglass of Irish whiskey.

Method: Use a long tumbler. Add the crushed mint and sugar to the soda water. When the sugar is dissolved the tumbler is filled with cracked ice and then – slowly and solemnly – the Irish whiskey is added. The julep is stirred until the glass has an elegant frost. Decorated with a sprig of mint, it can be sold by auction to the highest bidder.

Try an Irish Handshake too. You'll need two parts Irish whiskey, one part Green Curacao and one part fresh cream. Shake well with chipped ice and serve to guests who should take it on bended knee.

Quality

The Esquire Book of Drinks says, "Ireland is a country where . . . there isn't any bad liquor. In fact the general level . . . is Himalayan."

Transport Blarney

VISITORS TO IRELAND are fed into our transport system like sausage skins in a pork factory and emerge at the other end Blarney-stuffed. The variety of transport offered is very wide and each form offers its own distinct techniques and possibilities.

Dublin public transport is amiable enough but it is not personalized. They try to improve things on the organized tours but, no matter how noble the efforts of a courier, he must spread himself thin in the Plamas game and his main task is to create some form of collective Blarney. This chain-belt production line is all right in its own way, but put on your anti-Blarney armour when you fall into the hands of the Irish taxi-driver – particularly the Dublin species.

The Dublin Genie

Next to Baghdad's magic carpets you'll find the Irish taxi service amongst the world's best for instant service – at least in coming to the starting point. Reach for the telephone; dial the magic numbers and in an exhaust flash and a fairy cloud of carbon monoxide the thing is at the kerb. It is widely held that the Dublin taxi driver when he retires home – it is said his hours are from 7 a.m. to half-past exhaustion – is popped into a bottle like a genie by his ever-loving wife. One would not be surprised to find this is true.

He is, however, a solid character with certain resemblance to those busts of Socrates and Aristotle, that one sees in museums and art galleries. The resemblance does not end there; he is a real philosopher as well.

You are ready to go when he arrives but – hold it, friend – this is Ireland and we don't do things in that way. He gets out and examines your baggage. In fact he's reading it.

One imagines that the dearest wish of a Dublin taxi driver is to settle down before a big fire some evening, with a good selection of luggage and have a really good read of the labels. You urge him to movement and reluctantly he puts the things away. "And I never found out," he probably tells the wife, "how it ended."

Be Firm

"An' where would you be after going. Maybe 'tis that you would like to see the Phoenix Park or the Dublin mountains? Say the word and we're off."

Do not weaken. Do not yield to his infectious enthusiasm. Tell him you wish to go to your hotel.

"The Inter-Hibernian-Shelbourne-Gresham, is it? Very well, but we could take in the Phoenix Park and the Dublin Mountains on the way. You should look at them or you'll be sorry after. Tell you the truth I know them like the back of me hand. I do – honest."

Resist. It has been known for men and women to accept detours on their trip from the airport or railway station to their hotels and to arrive eight days later after quick glimpses of Connemara, Donegal and Kerry. Be firm at this stage – it pays. No, you wish to go to your hotel . . . you wish to go to your hotel . . . you wish to go to your hotel.

He relaxes. All that could be expected of him by the Taxi Owners' Association has been done.

At this point you might expect that subject A – the taxi driver – would usher subject B – the passenger – into the cab. Not so – and unseemly haste plays no part in the process.

Be Careful

"Would you be going to stay in the Inter-Hibernian-Shelbourne-Gresham Hotel?"

No harm will be done by admitting that this is your intention. Qualify your remark by pointing out that your use of the place is not unusual.

"I see (Begob) now. It's not a bad hotel but would you say it's as good as the hotels you've slept in outside Ireland?"

Careful. Once involved in a detailed comparison with prompts from your charioteer you may be whipped out to the Dublin mountains or the ruins of the medieval city of Glendalough with little for it at the end but a, "Well and weren't you talking so interestin' didn't I forget you didn't want to see the medieval city of Glendalough. Sure now that we're here we might as well look at it and maybe you'd like to see the Seven Wonders of Fore on the way back . . ."

Resist. Be careful. Press him to allow you the privilege of entering his cab. Indicate your weariness – speak of your fear that you may collapse but don't stress it too much or you'll find yourself doing a guided tour of the Dublin hospitals. "And here we have the Rotunda, the world's most famous maternity hospital . . ."

Keep off the subject of maternity also for Dublin's taxi drivers are trained in the art of midwifery and only the toughest stomach can take their lecture on "Umbiblical Hernias I have known with Clutch Sprocket Shearing noise."

It's a Small World . . .

You move off but you are conscious of his eyes on you in the driving mirror. He will almost open up the side of a bus like a sardine can and you wish he would stop looking backwards. He has assessed you and he now probes. Would you, by any chance, be from the United States/ England /Bechuanaland /Brazil /Malaya /Kuwait /Egypt or whatever other country your luggage labels and your accent suggests. You admit to the one of your choice.

The Irish taxi driver has a brother/a cousin/a son/a sister/ a friend/an acquaintance in whatever part of the world you come from.

Assume you admit to being from New York – a useful

deception if you're from Bradford – the probing will concentrate on that point.

"That's a coincidence entirely. Sure isn't it meself that has the cousin Liam Beag O Raghallaigh in New York. You will know of him surely for 'tis he is famous from one end of the city to the other."

Indicate coldly that Liam Beag O Raghallaigh is unknown at your end.

"He's a tall man is Liam Beag O Raghallaigh."

You know lots of tall men in New York.

"Do any of them know Liam Beag O Raghallaigh?"

Although your alarmed attention is focussed on the fact that the cab is shrinking with the spaces it goes through you confess they have never mentioned Liam Beag to you. To be fair you add that you never asked.

"New York now is an awful place for gangsters and murderers?"

You deny it with indignation and refer bitterly to baseless exaggeration. He will backtrack.

"You never said a truer word. Lies, lies, lies, lies. Sure the bloody Russians would damn any country with their propaganda. D'ye like it in Ireland?"

You are not here long enough to express an opinion but so far no one has thrown a brick at you.

"Wait, my good man, until they get friendly with you. I suppose you have Irish ancestors."

Disclaim any connection.

"No Irish relations? You're not one hundred per cent American then?"

Admit that your claim to be a true son of the Stars and Stripes is not so sound as it might have been had you the sense to have an Irish great-grandmother.

"Maybe," he'll comfort, "you had an Irish grandmother or grandfather and didn't know it."

The reflection on the morals of your nearest relations should be accepted; it is well-intentioned. He wishes to express his pity for you and to give you a little hope.

With effective anti-Blarney admire his driving and express the opinion that he does not appear to be the average taxi-man. Could this be so?

The Multiple-Expanding-Tip-Blarney

It is so. It is always so. Once you get him to expand on that topic he may drive you directly to your hotel before he finds out his mistake. It is the big Blarney gap in his defences. If you do succeed in getting him to drive you to your destination without further efforts to educate you in the ways and possessions of the Master Race he may be compelled to try the Unsolved-Mystery-Multiple-Expanding-Tip-Blarney on you which is reserved for special occasions.

He is pulling into the hotel entrance. Porters are hovering to seize your baggage and it is then he turns to you . . .

"Ye know, ever since you got into the cab there's something I wanted to say to you only I didn't like to, like . . ."

The menace and foreboding that can be injected into this is appalling. You slip him a portion of your wallet and ask for details.

"Just a moment now. I want to get that baggage out . . ."

You are out beside him. You slice your folding cash like a salami and press for information. Have you incipient symptoms of leprosy? Do you resemble someone wanted for murder? He has information that will alter your life?

"In a minute now . . . in a minute. Is this your sharkskin case?"

Yes, yes, yes, yes but speak, man, speak. You offer him the wallet. But in vain. It always is.

His radio is calling him urgently to a new assignment; a new traveller who may be crying out for guidance to the Dublin mountains or the medieval ruined city of Glenda-lough – he must away!

"Wait, wait . . ."

"Sorry, I've got to go. I'll run into you again. Don't forget to give my blessing to Liam Beag O Raghallaigh ..."
Yes, you will ... you will ... you will but speak, speak ...
Too late. He's gone.

And there you're left as countless others have been, with a mystery in your life that will never be solved. It has happened to thousands. Men wake screaming in Providence, Rhode Island as they remember it; women shrink with guilt in Leamington Spa with the echo of a Dublin taxi driver's words in their ear.

You may decide to search the city for the man – anything to bring peace of mind – but you'll never find him. He's either finished a novel or gone to sail around the world in a rowing boat. Taximen do not last. Better to seek out an old-time Irish jarvey and let him soothe your unquiet spirit.

Very Few of Them Left

The only real jarvey is one who drives an Irish Jaunting Car and there are few places where you will find him up on his extraordinary vehicle as it waddles along on two giant wheels. One place where both of them survive in all their glory is Killarney (Bedad). Not alone has the Irish Jaunting Car survived but the real antique, absolutely genuine Irish jarvey goes with it – a truly vintage product.

They bring to their work the thickest, slickest, smoothest, ball bearingist Blarney you're ever likely to know. If you can deal with Killarney Blarney, you can deal with anything.

The moment you step out of your train or car in the town beside the world's loveliest, mountain-ringed lakes a jarvey will materialize beside you. Materialize is the word. Like taximen, jarveys probably lurk in bottles waiting for the customer to turn up. One moment the man isn't there and the next you are staring into a broad, white-toothed grin while the words come in the soft honey-flow of the Co.

Kerry accent. *How* it is said is almost as important as *what* is said. There is heather, sunshine, the tumbling of clouds, the Atlantic flecked flavour of winds, the delicate call of sea birds, the hush of surf on the county's wide, sandy-warm beaches and much else in the voice that beguiles you and yours.

"Good day to you now and you'll be wanting a car to see the lakes – so you will. I'll take you now . . . and the lady too. You'd like that, lady? Arrah, climb up now and push that rug out of your way for I brought it in case you might find a touch of cold in the air after the long travelling. Mind up there – I'm talking to the horse, lady – Whoa!"

Resistance is Useless

You don't want to go but you cannot resist. You are in a trance and you try to stop yourself saying daft things like, "I hear, O Master, and I obey."

It is a debated point in Killarney pubs as to whether or not jarveys have a right to use force to compel visitors to go on jaunting cars. There is a minority school of thought which considers that the blunt instrument may be employed in case of refusal. To my mind these idle speculations are meaningless. No one refuses to go with a Killarney jarvey.

If you've never been on an Irish jaunting car before, the first glimpse may be a little startling. It is almost all wheels but on a clear day as you look up you can see the narrow plateau on which the passengers are supposed to sit. It soars before you like the more difficult sides of Mount Everest and you want to scream out that you are not related to Sir Edmund Hillary. Your worry about the height fades as the more alarming prospect of staying up when you get there, presents itself. After all Mount Everest stayed in the one spot when they were climbing it and didn't rock and sway along at ten miles an hour.

One way or another, you and your family are hauled into position above the six-foot wheels on to a tiny ledge where you sit facing out to the side and back to back with another group of passengers. All visitors to Killarney should pack a good-quality alpenstock in their baggage; it is very useful in mounting the jaunting car.

Screech if You Want Anything

When the passengers are in place, the jarvey climbs up and – like an amiable cocktail sausage between two pieces of rye bread – sits himself in a nice, safe, seat facing straight ahead.

You're off.

He stops, however, and puts you back as he realizes that you are the one who will pay for the others.

Once more you're off.

"Would you mind holding on to that bar there, sir, and you'll be all right. Are you feeling well, lady? Give a screech now if you want anything."

You bite your tongue before you can ask when the parachutes are issued and the thing is away. The camel has been described as the ship of the desert. In the same category the Irish jaunting car is the racing yacht of the roads. It floats and swings with pendulum movement, dipping and crashing through invisible rollers.

There is no record of the number of passengers lost off them each day but one can only wonder why the ditches of Killarney are not clogged with bewildered tourists trying to assemble themselves as the jarveys drive into the sunset blissfully unconscious that they've shed load.

"Over there, lady, is Muckross Abbey and now you'll not see the likes of it in your born life. Get up there, you stubborn mare – not you, lady, I mean, but the horse. They come from all over the world and I never heard anyone say he'd seen anything better in any part of the whole wide world. Isn't that a wonder entirely?"

Something Stirs . . .

One hangs on and inwardly compliments the Killarney visitor on his general discretion. You may wonder idly what would happen if anyone said the lakes were surpassed elsewhere but not for long. Something is happening in your interior. You can't guess what.

"Would you say now that you have anything at home that comes near Killarney in grandeur? What would you say to that?"

You know you are in the hands of the Irish Master Race. They have you on a jaunting car and you recall their Neolithic blood group and their dilute Nordic plasma – you betray the land of your birth. The chorus obediently rings out from the passengers.

"No, nothing in America/England/Saudi Arabia/Thailand/Monaco/etc. equals this."

"Ye all surely have the right of it."

He is satisfied. You have confirmed the truth as countless others have in the past and innumerable others will in the future.

By this time you feel a funny numbness in the depths of your digestive system. It spreads. A horrible nausea erupts and you realize that you are seasick.

. . . You've Never Lived

Ghastly as it is, it is reduced to minor importance by the sudden, unreasonable fear of shipwreck. Why, you groan to yourself, does this damn jaunting car not have lifeboats? What are the maritime authorities doing about it and it is not equipped, contrary to international law, with flush scuttles or fiddley ventilators.

This is all delirium but you reach some imaginary harbour before you finally break down and as you are carried down a mirage of a gangplank you hear anchors crash down into the grass.

Write it off as a valuable experience and there is nothing like it in this satiated world. No one has lived fully until he or she has ridden with a Killarney jarvey.

The Viking Boatmen

Boatmen in Ireland are not merely jarveys with oars or outboard motors. They are a tougher breed and much less given to Blarney. One suspects that they are descended from the Vikings. If you want to see what they can be like in their most exotic form dash off to Glengarriff where they ferry passengers to and from Garnish Island, a sub-tropical paradise about five hundred yards from shore – a place made for Hawaiian maidens with its flower-rainbowed gardens of fragrance.

You arrive in Glengarriff at 11.00 hours and at 11.01 hours you are on your way to Garnish in the middle of a press-ganged group of tourists who weep openly at the prospect of being separated from their relatives and friends for a long time. Even if you have been over to the island five minutes previously you can just as easily be conscripted again.

One timid little Hampstead pet shop owner – a meek and humble species – travelled backwards and forwards for two weeks before he was rescued by force.

One cannot withhold admiration from the Garnish Island boatmen – there are a few weak-kneed amongst them who lack backbone and request people to go with them but they are on the liquidation list – who preserve the highest standards of the ancient Irish sea kings in all their splendid glory.

Get a Garnish Island boatman in the relaxed atmosphere of the local in the evening and he is quite likely to speak bitterly of the decline of the galleys of another era when you could chain your tourists to the oar. He hints that dangerous liberalism of this kind is likely to undermine civilization.

The Floating Jarveys

The Connemara boatmen are a different breed and they are essentially floating jarveys. Big and kindly they will softly urge you to test the thrill of a trip in a currach.

"'Tis a great day surely to be after going out past the mouth of the sea and to take the high sport of the waves. Let ye be coming now while the hand of the saints is pressing down the wildness of the water's bosom."

Let's be fair – currach sailing is the nearest thing to Russian roulette you'll find in Ireland. But Blarneyed you'll be into trying it so you should be warned.

A currach is a boat constructed of canvas, wooden laths and faith in the saints of Heaven that do be pressing down the wildness of the waters' bosom. It is Europe's most primitive surviving craft. *It* has survived – will you? Tarred all over, it looks like a filleted shark and you don't get into it – you are swallowed. It will be a painless experience initially, for the Connemara boatmen will make it seem the easiest thing in the world to go out to sea with them.

"A grand day is in it, thank God, for putting out to the gentleness of the big ocean."

It seems impossible to get into a currach without putting your foot through its cardboard-thin side but miracles strew your path all the way in Ireland and you are in as someone from shore pushes it off leaving you to look at a couple of deep-bronzed men with wide grins pretending to row and control the thing.

You now experience what it is like to be a table tennis ball as the waves tap you and the currach backwards and forwards. You pity table tennis balls.

"Isn't it too rough?" you shout as your stomach swings like a digestive pendulum.

"'Tis only middlin' rough," the beguiling liquid voices flow back, "'Twas worse earlier."

You'll Not Die – This Time . . .

You are not consoled. Now you find that the damn thing has the power to stand upright at right angles to the water. In a moment of your agony you are convinced the thing is looping the loop.

"Shouldn't we turn back," you yell and wish the currach would steady enough to let you get violently sick.

"Have no fear on you. 'Tis Michael and meself will keep you from the harm of the ocean. You'll not die this time."

You wonder if this is a consolation and one passenger is reported to have said in reply to a similar remark, "It's the hope of dying that's keeping me alive."

Words are no longer of any value.

You wonder if your affairs are in order and contemplate throwing yourself into the sea it could be safer than the currach. Just at that moment they bring it up on to the soft white sands of the beach and lay you down. You hang on to the sand – no one can be too careful.

"And didn't you like it now?" they'll ask, grinning from under caps with peaks like cinema canopies.

"And is it you would be after going out fishing now that you know the ways of the currach?"

In your heart you wonder if this is Blarney to make you buy a space in the local cemetery but they are kindly people and they aid you to the nearest public house. A large Irish whiskey flows through your bloodstream and you recover a little – enough to resist the temptation to lie on the floor.

Nonetheless it takes a few days to be normal again and to be immune to the Blarney assaults of those who sell souvenirs in the West. One man we heard of bought seven hundredweight of Connemara marble paper weights in the twenty-four hours after a currach trip. Today he has the most unusual garden rockery in Wigan.

Dracula was Irish

BRAM STOKER, the author of *Dracula*, was an Irishman who was born at 15, The Crescent, Clontarf, Dublin, in November 1847, the son of a civil servant. He himself became a civil servant and indeed a bestseller of his which has not been reprinted in modern times was "The Rules of the Clerks of the Petty Sessions in Ireland".

Early in life he became interested in journalism and he was one of Dublin's leading theatre critics. A friend of Oscar Wilde and his family, he was a well known figure in the city. He met Henry Irving in Dublin and within a short time became his manager, a post he held until Irving's death. He exhausted himself with work. Running the affairs of the Lyceum Theatre he wrote as many as fifty letters a day in longhand.

This did not prevent him writing and in 1897 he turned out his most famous work, *Dracula*. Its success was enormous and as a play it continues to meet with public response. Stoker died in April, 1912, having left his mark on the British theatre no less than on the history of Gothic fiction.

Loo Valley and Elsewhere

THERE ARE MANY places in Ireland with delightful names, but few so suggestive or so romantic as the Loo Valley near Killarney. Most visitors seem to think it a magnificent idea to give such a name to this well-watered glen with its tempting nooks and inviting bushes. But the Loo Valley is not the only place in Ireland with a pleasant name. Indeed there is poetry in almost every townland.

What suggestions of the Can-Can and Paris are to be found in the name of that Co. Limerick village, Oola. Then there is Emo which, for some reason, reminds people of Australia.

If anyone ever wants to hold an international convention for publicity organizations, surely they needn't look any further than Ballyhoo, which is near Waterford City. Visiting Russians can make pilgrimage to Moscow in Co. Laois, but they should avoid Siberia in Co. Sligo. Co. Louth has Piedmont and Co. Kilkenny offers Geneva, Shanghai and Van Diemen's Land. Co. Sligo has Gibraltar and the original Coney Island is there also.

Pass, Shirtless Servant

The longest name in Irish topography is a matter of dispute, but Castletownconyersmaceniery in Co. Limerick has a strong claim to the title. Also strong in the running is

Muickeenachidirdhashaile. If you ever had an afternoon to spare you might like to try and pronounce that last one and a rough phonetic equivalent is "Muck - heen - idge - er - daw - sawl - yeh". Championed by many, Cooneenaskirroogohifran (little harbour sliding to Hell) suffers from one handicap – no one has ever established that it exists. In Co. Donegal they offer Bealachanghiollaganleine (the pass of the shirtless servant).

Wart Cure

A VERY SUCCESSFUL Blarney cure for warts, which is almost always successful, is to rub the growth with the cut face of a potato that has been dipped in fresh rain water. It should be rubbed up and down seven times. Don't ask how or why it works – be happy that it does and remember that the Irish are one of the most unwarty races in the world.

International Blarney

IT IS A Blarney principle that truth is too important to be dependent on such things as facts. It has a particular application to the Irish world view. If you want to understand us and our image of the universe you will have to accept that where reality contradicts Blarney-truth, all one can say sympathetically is – Heaven help reality.

Looking at Ireland, we see that it covers two-thirds of the earth's surface (never mind geography or surveyors). It is the complete centre of world attention. Eskimos cannot start the day until they hear the latest from Sligo; the Soviet Government tosses in its sleep at night wondering what attitude the Irish Government will take to its actions. Cannibals in New Guinea go off their food with worry when they hear of a Dublin cyclist falling on his way home to Ballyfermot and the development of the transistor set is attributed to the need for the world's population to keep in instant touch with what is going on in Connemara. Once you grasp this simple Blarney truth you are well on your way to understanding us.

The B.B.B.S.

Many people envy us – particularly a mysterious and unlocated race known as the Base, Brutal and Bloody Saxon and we've got to keep our eyes open at all times for this

dangerous B.B.B.S. It would be wrong to imagine that we associate the Base, Brutal and Bloody with the English – far from it. All the English visiting us are obviously fine, decent, upright (except after an adequate intake of good Irish whiskey) men and women who couldn't by any stretch of the imagination be called B.B.B.S. The unholy illegitimates exist just the same and you have to get up early in the morning – well, not too early – to foil their foul, fallacious, fantastic felonies.

With that splendid generosity that you would expect of an open-handed race – warm in its generosity and hot in its leather – the Irish are quite happy to allot one-third of their world image to Britain and the United States with their

Canadian, Australian and New Zealand suburbs. The existence of foreign countries is permitted at regular intervals but we can't allow them any part of the globe. They have a sort of perpendicular existence at right angles to the Straits of Dover. This is a major cause of seasickness in the English Channel.

In our world image, as I say, we grant one-third of the globe to the unfortunate non-Irish. This is partly philanthrophy, but also it permits us to have an audience. What's the use of being the noblest, the most intelligent, the bravest, the kindest and the most extraordinary race of beings that ever knew life, if there's no one around to recognize the fact? We know our virtues and even though we blush – we are the most modest people breathing – we like someone to endorse it.

Pity the Non-Irish

Indeed we are kind enough to pity those who are not one of ourselves. For instance an English lecturer wanted to show a Co. Cork audience what he thought of his nationality and he asserted, "I was born an Englishman, I live an Englishman and I'll die an Englishman."

From the audience came a genuine cry of horror, "Be the heroic trousers of the great Finn McCool himself – have you no ambition in you at all?"

In our Blarney world picture the nations expand or contract with the heat of world tension. Russia when out of the news shrinks to the immediate area in the vicinity of Moscow and even this status is a concession by the Irish. When, however, the Soviet Union is reaching out for a handful of uranium, with every indication of throwing it at the world, the country expands until it overshadows the sky, causes rain in Connemara and puts lighting-up time forward by about two gloomy hours.

China, on the other hand, has no tangible existence. Unlike Texas, however, which is a complete myth dreamed up by the American advertising industry – it is around somewhere. It could be considered as a sort of bacteria – everywhere but nowhere. You have to be careful of it even though you can't see or touch it and if you get a cut finger watch out for Peking infection.

The Fertile Irish Bicycle

One of the reasons we feel so kindly to the English is the fact that they ruled us for seven hundred years. We are certain they are now overcome by remorse and desire to atone for their terrible deeds –the poor spalpeens. Of course – like the Americans – it is also assumed that the English are overflowing with Irish blood, something that indicates the stamina of the sons of Ireland.

There is a story of a Co. Galway labourer who fathered vast numbers of children in the English Midlands – much to his surprise, let it be recorded. His confessor was shocked and asked: "How can you possibly do it?"

"Well, Father," replied the sinner, "I've got to admit, and may the Devil damn the machine, that I had a bicycle."

In view of the vast array of Irish grandparents claimed by English people it is suspected that one or two Irishmen were using a tandem. Evidence for the fertility of the Irish bicycle can be found in the United States as well.

If anyone doubts our uniqueness – and only the Base, Brutal and Bloodies would–it must be pointed out that not one ambassador sent to Ireland has a word to say against us. They get up there and tell us how much the Japanese admire us; how the Indians think we are the nearest thing to sacred cows and how the Spaniards wouldn't swop us for garlic. With that sort of evidence can anyone question our genius?

Of course we praise other countries but that's different – everything is, in Ireland. We realize how tough it must be to wake up in the morning and remember that you are not Irish and so we jolly everyone else along as best we can.

Indeed, all Blarney could be said to spring from that sympathy.

We, the Master Race, pity you, World.

The Irish Occupation of England

England – which in Blarney geography consists of London, Birmingham, Liverpool and Coventry – has a very special place in our thinking. Out of it came those Base, Brutal and Bloody Saxons who occupied us for seven hundred long years. This gives it a warm place in our affections particularly as the Irish are going to occupy England – it has already started – and it will be our turn for the next seven hundred years. Watch it, mate!

We also expect gratitude from the Americans and the British – and the French should remember that General de Gaulle had Irish grandparents – because of our generosity in emigrating to their countries and giving them presidents, generals and politicians. Sure and didn't we build up their economies and their political institutions? We don't want to harp on this but we expect it to be a proper background to the attitude of the Americans and the British to us. We've earned their gratitude.

Looked at through the Blarney haze, all Americans with no Irish connections are classified as honorary millionaires with the right – and duty – to toss dollars to the right and left impartially. Anything they claim about their personal prosperity is accepted without question, but nothing else is to be believed. Americans exaggerate everything. They even expect us to believe in Texas.

Who Believes in Texas?

For Americans, Texas is a sort of Tir nan Og – a fairyland where all dreams come true. No doubt psychologists and sociologists could explain the need of the United States for a myth of this kind but it should be strictly reserved for home consumption. Texas – indeed! If we believed in that place they'd expect us to accept California as well. Normally we Irish treat these whoppers with a tactful Blarney silence. But don't always depend on our patience.

Americans are the world's greatest moaners. They complain that the central heating isn't hot enough and even when there's no central heating they complain about that. 'Tis a way they have with it and you do be after having to butter them with Blarney to the heels of their blessed feet to keep them quiet a little.

Don't I know of one poor Co. Kerry hotel owner who gave Americans the best room in his house – one with a bath and shower? Have ye any idea of what they complained of? No water in the shower, no less.

Sure if there was no shower there couldn't be any water so why bother a man who goes to the trouble of at least giving them the shower itself?

So Why Was it After Smelling?

The English don't complain much, but when they do they have a fearful way of making their complaints to the right people, and they do be nasty enough to write to the tourist authorities in Dublin. This brings big, black-faced, stern men down on top of the poor hotel owners and they to be asking why the bill is so high or why the boiled egg was after smelling?

When Americans complain they always do it properly and call for the manager who is on the side of the man who employs him – as a decent man should be. Nice and proper too but the thought of doing anything that might come between the proud Saxon and his fruit juice, cereal, toast, bacon, eggs and sausages gives grey hairs to even the baldest of our hotel proprietors.

Foreigners – the non-American and non-English population of the world – are human it is now generally accepted in Ireland. Maybe there is a school of thought that looks on them as humanoid – something like the artificial men of science fiction – but this is only partially correct.

They have to be heavily Blarneyed and the best way is to let them do all the talking. When they slow down we refuel their conversational powers with an odd "Glory be to the saints of the Holy City of Clonmacnoise", or a simple, "And do you tell me now that Paris is as big as the village of Ballynascubeen?"

The German Take-Over

Foreigners eat snails, drink olive oil and are hopelessly immoral and they couldn't be trusted alone with a female oyster even when there's an "R" in the month. Given the chance they will carry on shamelessly with any woman they can – the lucky unmentionables.

The Germans – it is held in Ireland – have abandoned their own country to take over all the best beaches in Ireland. In time they will be absorbed by the native population and this will top up our blood-stream with a fresh Nordic splash. It's a pity to see it happen and Germany could have continued to exist but with the language they have they were losing a lot through lockjaw. It may add a few long-herred (copyright) intellectuals to our society.

Altogether we can convey the consoling message to the non-Irish that they will continue to be tolerated. Once we are recognized as the supreme and ultimate Master Race there should be no difficulty.

The Franco-Irish Revolution

IT IS NOT a joke or an exaggeration to make the claim that the Seagreen Incorruptible of the French Revolution, Maximilien Francois Marie Isidore de Robespierre was of Irish origin. The man who created the Terror was born at Arras and it was a well-established tradition in the area that the family came from Ireland. Dr. Richard Hayes, a distinguished scholar, concludes that the family came from Kilkenny where their name was Roth Fitz Piere.

Whatever the basis of Robespierre's Irish connections, there can be no doubt about the contribution of the race to the French Revolution. The attack on the Bastille was led by an Irishman, James Blackwell. The chaplain of the place was an Irish priest, the Abbe MacMahon, and the first prisoner to be released was another son of Erin, Francis Xavier Whyte. French Revolution, how are you?

St. Patrick was British

IT IS A sad fact that the patron saint of Ireland was British and no one seriously doubts now that St. Patrick came from the homeland of the Base, Brutal and Bloody. His father was a clergyman and so, too, was his grandfather.

The Green Ray

IN ONE OF his novels Jules Verne, the French author, writes of a professor who came to Galway Bay to see the phenomenon of the Green Ray. As he looked out to sea at sunset a boat sailed across the horizon and spoiled his view of the last tip of light as the sun went down. He left the place in disgust but he was a cloth-headed idiot to do so as the west coast of Ireland offers the best opportunities in Europe for observing the Green Ray.

It is seen as the sun sets behind a distant horizon in calm, clear air. As the last edge of the sun's disc goes down there is a sudden green or green-blue flash of great purity. It lasts for only seconds but it is a fascinating spectacle. It can also be seen at sunrise but who is going to get up in time?

The explanation lies in the fact that the atmosphere acts as a prism and disperses the light in the spectrum. Since green and blue are refracted more than red they are the last colours to be seen as the sun vanishes.

Irish Skis

It was an Irishman, Sir Arthur Conan Doyle who introduced the sport of ski-ing to Switzerland. Of course he also
became famous as the creator of Sherlock Holmes. His wife
suffered from tuberculosis and he took her to the drier air of
the Alps. He brought with him several pairs of Norwegian
skis and tumbled around the snowy slopes of Davos. The
visitors laughed at him and laughed even more when he
asserted stubbornly that one day there would be thousands
following in his boots.

Once he led two Swiss across the Furha Pass to Arosa
and finished the last few miles on the seat of his pants.
John Dickson Carr has told the whole story in his life of
Sir Arthur. His uncle Henry Doyle became Director of the
National Gallery in Dublin and bought so cheaply and
wisely that the collection which he helped create is today
worth about fifty million pounds or more and is one of the
best in Europe.

Drinking Blarney

DRINKING in Ireland is often a vocation and a profession. Strong men set their jaws early in life and vow that they will be bigger, better, wider, longer and, if possible, deeper drinkers than their fathers.

Statistically it is calculated that 109.6729 per cent succeed.

Everything is soluble in Irish whiskey, gin, porter or stout – genius, troubles, joys, talent, bankruptcy and anything else you like to contemplate. On any day in Dublin's public houses you will find large numbers of strong silent men who, faced with the fact that they can't afford to drink, are comforting themselves with glasses of Irish whiskey.

Since a lot of Blarney is served with alcohol in Ireland you should know a little of the background.

Sometimes, to hear the legends you'd think that the country was an alcoholics' paradise. Where else, it might be asked will you find towns with one public house or saloon to every five drinkers of the population. True there are not many of these, but they exist. Taking the country as a whole there is about one public house or saloon to every sixty drinkers which doesn't indicate any danger of people dying of thirst.

Remember the Children

It is no wonder then that strong men coming to us for the first time are inclined to brace their steel wills in case they'll be Blarneyed into wild drunkenness. They drink huge quantities of milk to offset the intake of alcohol into their bloodstream and their wives plead with them to remember the children. They needn't worry – the Irish drink no more and often drink less than people in other countries. As Robert Lynd wrote in one of his essays, the Irish are always more vividly drunk than anyone else – they have a talent for it that is given to few. This gives the impression that they are great drinkers.

It must be recorded, too, that we have more devoted non-drinkers of alcohol than any other Western country. They wear badges and flaunt the fact that they are proud of their abstinence. Every year they gather in thousands and denounce drink and drinkers. It is fortunate that the drink in the country is so good or the obstacles would make us drier than a Muslim mosque.

The drinkers do not counter-attack and treat the militant non-drinkers with pity. As one of them remarked, "Wouldn't your heart bleed for these unfortunates. Isn't it an awful thing for a teetotaller to wake up in the morning and know he'll never feel any better?" At one time an organization called Alcoholics Unanimous was established in Dublin but its membership fell away and it wasn't worth while to prop them up against the bar counters again.

The Hairy Balladeers

Drinking and music in Ireland go together quite a bit and almost every second lounge or bar has its resident ballad group or hires them by the night. The Irish ballad singer tends to run to hair and it has been calculated that it would be a poor group that wouldn't provide enough to stuff a mattress if ever they allowed themselves to be separated from it.

Private singing by the customers is carried on in a few places but it is considered bad manners for anyone to join in a song they didn't start. While "Nellie Dean" is exclusively

belted out in one corner, extracts from "The Desert Song" are being lashed out elsewhere but never the twain shall meet.

Do not therefore, lightly twang a vocal cord in harmony with singers in your vicinity. They are likely to stop in the middle of a semibreve and look you sharply in the eye. Courteous conversation for a while will always result in an invitation to share an odd *arpeggio* or a *pianissimo* but the etiquette demands that you wait for it.

With all the temptations that beset his path, and the influence of modern economics, it is difficult at times for the Irish to keep drinking. It is particularly hard when the legal tender is not to hand and the fear of dying of thirst grips the throat with a black, dry hand. Such a situation calls for emergency measures. You can turn to your friends but quite often you catch them on the financial roundabout as they turn to you.

Thanks to St. Patrick – who brought distilling to us – the condition is rare. There are many methods to be used in extreme cases and one is the Where-Have-You-Been-Mick-All-This-Time-And-Come-Up-And-See-The-Wife-And-Me-Tonight-Blarney. The form of the invitation is vital for it is little more than an extended and decorative version of the British Delicate Hint.

The Loaded Invitation

"You'll come up, me oul' segocia. Sure, you put the heart in the lot of us and the way things are going don't we need the oul' laugh and who can tell a story better. The wife is dying to see you again and she nearly got the heart flutters at the jokes the last time."

The Victim blushes. He knows he's good but why should anyone else tell him so. He agrees to go and see the family of the Blarneyite. He will tell funny stories and amuse the wife.

"That's great, Mick. D'you know how to get there?"

The Victim has been there before and can find his way.

"Wait, Mick, I'll tell you. Be careful when you come to the garden gate and when you push it with your shoulder, mind you don't tear the coat on the latch."

The Victim expresses agreement that the tearing of his coat on the latch would be undesirable.

"Come round to the side of the house, Mick, and push the side door with your shoulder and it'll open. When you come to the back, watch the branch of the ash tree and push it to one side with your shoulder and the back door will go easy if you shove it with the elbow. You're sure to come now? You won't let us down?"

The Victim is grateful. He will not let them down. He will tell his stories – but he is curious.

"What's all this pushing gates with my shoulder and shoving in backdoors with my elbow?" he'll ask, as it has been planned he should. The jaws of the trap snap.

"Ah Mick, how else would you do it and you with the dozen bottles of stout under each arm?"

The Irish Touch

The stranger in our midst is, of course, a special gift from the Gods who must not be neglected and some Irish citizens will treat him as a perambulating oasis. *Some* Irish citizens, let it be noted, for although the dedicated "toucher" is rare in Ireland, he is to be found in close proximity to alcohol more often than anywhere else.

Of course the atmosphere of our public houses, particularly in the cities, will condition the Victim to generosity. These public houses are sometimes described in tourist literature as ". . . havens of old-world charm where the visitor is amused and delighted by the sparkle of witty, intellectual and richly native conversation."

When he enters, he will hear all around him the music of great pints of stout or golden goblets of whiskey as they ripple over and break on well-seasoned tonsils. Nearby, the strains of a ballad – filtered through vast layers of hair – will cheerfully describe the hanging of some Irish hero or else indicate the desirability of giving some red-coated British lackey an injection of a fifteen foot pike. Musically the Irish public houses are amiable hotbeds of revolution.

Scraps of Witty, Intellectual and Richly Native conversation – abbreviated to WIRN – will drift to his ears.

". . . an' I said to him, I said, 'I hope St. Peter himself finds time to reach through the rafters of Heaven to give you a kick in the side of the skull.' I tell you this. He didn't like it . . ."

"... that illegitimate is so mean he wouldn't give you a slide if he owned the Alps ..."

"Foreigners is very ignorant. Very ignorant, Jem. The last voyage we put in to Barcelona and would you believe some of them fellas hadn't heard we'd got rid of the trams in Dublin. I ask you ... they didn't even know that much. Just imagine not knowin' that in Barcelona ..."

Thus it will go on.

Hello Again ...

The techniques used to cast you as Moses' Rock will be many, but one which derives from the Unsolved-Mystery-Multiple-Expanding-Tip-Blarney is to be guarded against. This is the Well-There-You-Are-Again-And-Sober-As-A-Teetotaller's-Camel-Blarney.

The speed and dash of this attack is all important and the Victim can scarcely get time to think as his hand is pumped like a bilge pump. His thoughts are stampeded – and he is often selected because he obviously has a blood-stream diluted by alcohol.

"Where – I mean – when ...?"

The Thirst is shocked. You don't remember – you can't tell when the foundation of this great friendship was laid?

"Go on," he'll say. "Have a guess and remember the last time you waded up to your hips in drink."

"At the Shelbourne?" you ask with a disturbed conscience, or you give some other information of use to the Thirst. He weighs the reply in the scales of utility.

"Of course, it was the Shelbourne." He has detected the quaver of guilt with a psychological radar. He has you.

"I don't remember much about it ..." the Victim may excuse.

"Just as well," the Thirst will answer with tones as dark as Guinness. He invests the remark with a suggestion of terrible deeds best forgotten unless the police raise the matter. He does it well with a sense of horror that befits a citizen of the land that produced Dracula (see page 90).

Was It the Blonde?

The Victim is disturbed. He can't remember too clearly what happened but there was the large blonde who stood up suddenly and said something rather nasty about his conduct. It hadn't mattered at the time but the whole thing was so vague in the memory that it could mean anything. Once his mind gets on that blonde he is compelled to find out.

"Was it anything to do with the large blonde?"

The Thirst wraps his ears around each remark like gift paper. Authenticity; genuine anxiety – that's what he's after. He recognizes it for what it is. Concern.

"Of course . . . of course . . . who else?"

The Victim is now anxious. Very Anxious.

"Look . . . I say . . . er . . . what's the name?"

"Mean to say," asserts the Thirst indignantly, "that you don't even remember my name when it was me got you out of the place before the Hall Porter came? Mean to say you don't know my name's Paddy?"

The Victim wilts. This is getting serious.

"Of course, I do, Paddy. Of course. But look, about this . . . wait, will you have a drink first? What do you drink?"

The Thirst allows a vision of melted boot polish, turpentine, eau de cologne and paint remover to pass before his mind.

"Well, at this time of the day I usually stick to a ball of malt. Irish."

"I see. You want a large Irish whiskey?"

The Thirst is indignant.

"Lookit now," he asserts with the air of a man who is going to finally nail a lying slander, "there is no such thing as a large Irish whiskey – and its been said often enough – but a big glass will help."

The Thirst – and he is a multitude – will be doing very badly if he fails to spend the rest of the evening in liquid comfort. With sufficient skill he might be able to make one or two evenings out of the strange tale of What Actually Happened At The Shelbourne.

The Mass Touch

This is a basic Well-There-You-Are-And-As-Sober-As-A-Teetotaller's-Camel-Blarney but it has many different forms. It can also be used for a mass "touch" and the sympathy of a well-organized Irish group of citizens will put grey hairs on a bald man's head as they tell him of the catastrophes they pray he'll avoid. Supported by such sympathy even the tightest wallet will swing open on rusty hinges to be liquidated.

Since drink provides inspiration, you will find certain pubs in Ireland where the novelists, playwrights, poets and writers are to be found diligently and tirelessly searching for ideas at the bottom of glasses. Indeed, if they could spare the time from drinking they might write something.

They are so closely packed in these places, one Irish writer has stated that if you spit into one of them you can't miss a poet. Why poets should be in the way all the time is not explained.

You will almost certainly be impressed by the range of knowledge displayed and the up-to-date acquaintance of most writers with world literary trends. You will need to know the secret of much of this literary Blarney.

The Literary Blarney

An important section of the Irish public has made the discovery that the reading of books is a complete waste of time. They find that if you read the critics in the better-quality magazines and newspapers you can be absolutely brilliant. Not alone do you have a detailed insight to the contents of the book but you know the right things to say about it.

If anyone interested in culture is coming to join us for a spell he should check up on the latest trends and fashions in

the arts. Words like "catharsis", "soul" and "commit-
ment" should be thrown around like confetti. "Soul" is
particularly important and you can flavour it now and then
with a reference to "a feeling for life" or "an awareness of
significance in the Celtic ethos". This will give you a fairly
strong position in literary Blarney. Now and then but not
too often rattle off something like "The Celtic *Weltan-
schauung* has a discrete continuum . . ." This goes down big.

Literary pubs are usually crowded and some 58.6794 per
cent of the population is writing; is going to write or has
written the Great Definitive Work of Irish Literature. The
writers will be all about you – some tossed over the counter
like old rugs and others folded in chairs like a spinster's
nightie. WIRN will be everywhere. WIRN, of course, is
witty, intellectual and richly native conversation.

If you wish to mix with the Irish literary set, try and
remember that it is cheapest to stick to Abbey playwrights.
They dispense WIRN on a diet of pints or bottles of stout.
Novelists are normally reasonable although if they have
written a novel which, "expresses the Celtic dilemma in the
atomic age" or one which ". . . explores man's situation in
the tragic metaphysical realism of our time" he may come
expensive. Poets are quite dangerous and they may look for
saki, brandy or tequila. But after all you are in the land that
produced James Joyce, Anthony Butler, Sean O'Casey,
Anthony Butler, William Butler Yeats, Anthony Butler and
many others including, Anthony Butler, and you must expect to pay for your WIRN.

The Flowing Bowl

It has been contended that visitors to Ireland will never
learn to Blarney drink from the natives on any significant
scale and no general method that can be suggested is likely
to have much success. On the other hand there are what one
might call institutional opportunities to find a place at the
drinking trough.

This involves what is known as the This-Is-One-Reception-I-Couldn't- Miss-And-Thanks-For-The-Invitation-Blarney. On any given day Dublin's hotels are packed tight with organizations holding receptions at which vast quantities of drink flows generously and – most important of all – freely. The visitor can usually find these events listed in the hotels.

A few discreet inquiries, a little brushing up of knowledge, and he or she can walk straight into the flowing bowl. Many of the organizers of these events are often quite desperate for guests and do not inquire too closely into the status of those who wander in. They are grateful for the loan of their presence which helps to swell the numbers. All this requires is iron nerve and the smooth word. The moment anyone approaches with a puzzled brow and tentative inquiries the correct procedure is to grab his hand firmly: look him straight in the eye and say, "This was one reception I couldn't miss and thank you for the invitation. Do join me in a drink. Waiter!"

If he still coughs and hums his way towards more information you push a glass into his hand and with an air of shocked surprise make a counter-query, "I don't think you know me? I'm John Doe – does that strike a chord?"

He won't dare admit it doesn't, but as he mumbles with confusion you clinch the matter with the announcement, "I suppose you could call me – *the* John Doe." After this you will have little more to do than accept his apologies for not having recognized your name and there will be no further trouble.

The Guinness-Go-Round

Although the system mentioned is the best way to ease yourself towards a regular intake of alcohol it does require skill and verbal polish. Lesser breeds may like to try other methods which, though lacking finesse, place less strain on the visitor's nerve.

The larger brewers in Dublin will gladly lead herds of visitors about their premises and ply them with literature. At the end of the trip they normally hand out a sample of their products. One is easy to obtain and to get it you lend yourself to their guides for a short while, but how does one establish a claim on the second?

The simplest gimmick is – disguise. Little more than a large suitcase (about two feet by three feet has been found useful) is required in which to keep your make-up kit, your wigs, false beards, moustaches and your changes of clothes. Go around the brewery once and take your first free drink. Then retire somewhere and change into a new costume. Around the brewery again and another free drink. If I may be allowed a little Atmospheric Warp it can be said that you will surely be having the big black bubbles blowing from your ears and the help of St. Patrick to be keeping you on your feet.

Musha, Bedad and Begob, this alcoholic merry-go-round requires a little Blarney skill to confuse and evade the suspicions of the officials. If one of them discovers a close resemblance between the Serbo-Croat Folk Dancer in embroidered waistcoat who holds out a thirsty hand and the turbaned Sikh of twenty minutes before – a smooth and well-applied word may be necessary.

Tracing Ali Singh

The Serbo-Croat Folk Dancer should become very agitated about his cousin, Ali Singh, who has gone on ahead of him. He will draw the attention of the official to the fact that they both look alike and suggest this may aid in tracing the missing one. This is almost certain to work and, properly handled, could obtain a second tankard straight away to soothe the nerves. Arthur Guinness and his sons are most reluctant to obtain a reputation of mislaying the Sikh cousins of Serbo-Croat Folk Dancers. If it got around it could give them a bad name.

On your next trip you should use a heavy beard and dark glasses and cast yourself in the part of an ancient Spanish aristocrat with a severe speech impediment. There's no use taking risks.

There is a rumour that one disguised Dubliner has been going around Guinness's brewery for the past twenty-seven years, man and boy, and has never gone home sober. This is an inspiring devotion to a noble cause but it shows what can be done. Of course there are more drastic and cruder systems. Fainting outside public houses has almost exhausted the charity of the proprietors, but in times of stress one may still see littered pavements outside some premises with a repute for generosity.

. . . And Make Them Large Ones

A bricklayer of our acquaintance will in desperation throw himself off building scaffolds in order to be revived by a glass of spirits. On one occasion he gave his usual performance and was shocked to hear the foreman shout, "Quick, get him a drink of water!"

"Here," he protested indignantly, "how far do you have to fall to get a glass of whiskey?"

At the same time he is ready to take advantage of any dialogue that aids his cause. On another occasion he fell from the scaffold and the foreman cried, "Bring him to – bring him to!"

With unerring opportunism he sat up and whispered hoarsely, "And make both of them large whiskies."

One does not commend these methods to everyone – they are the specialized tactics of a master.

The Natterjack Toad

SNAKES AND REPTILES do not exist in Ireland, but not because of St. Patrick. The scientific theory is that both Ireland and England were once part of the European mainland. Ireland, with that fierce independence which is her great virtue, was the first to cut the link with the continent.

As the Ice Age ended – sometime around August, 5000 B.C., although the month isn't certain – the reptiles came northwards. When they arrived in Britain they found that Ireland had gone in July 8000 B.C. and since there was no air service they had to stay where they were.

At a much later time the Natterjack Toad did get into the country and managed to establish a foothold in the subtropical climate of south Co. Kerry, attracted no doubt by the absolute beauty of the Dingle peninsula. Although it looks like a frog it walks instead of hopping and it has – one regrets admitting it – a distinct odour.

It is true that we also have the frog and the Triturus vulgaris or Common Newt but at least their moral character is above reproach. We don't like talking about it – particularly in front of the children – but the conduct of the Natterjack Toad at mating time is Casanova-like. It was ruthlessly exposed in the *1930* edition of Chambers Encyclopedia – which pointed out that it was "very prolonged in its sexual embraces". We don't want that sort of thing, particularly at the end of the Dingle peninsula.

Betsy's Cocktail

THERE ARE MANY explanations for the origin of the cocktail, but the one generally accepted gives the credit to Betsy Flannagan, a lady innkeeper during the period of the American War of Independence. The customers at her Four Corners Tavern were mainly officers of Washington's Army and one night she served an inventive mixture of rum, rye and fruit juices, decorating each glass with a cock's feather.

"Hurrah for the cock's tail," shouted one of the delighted soldiers and history was made.

Poor Man's Irish Coffee

MOST PEOPLE by now know how to make Irish Coffee, but few have heard of the beverage made with Guinness. The coffee is made in the usual way but instead of water you use the good black stout of Ireland. Delicious hot or cold, with sugar or without, topped with whipped cream or not.

If you don't know how to make the real Irish coffee you'll need, Cream rich as an Irish brogue, Coffee strong as a friendly hand, Sugar sweet as the tongue of a rogue, Whiskey smooth as the wit of the land.

Heat a stemmed whiskey glass. Pour in one shot of Irish whiskey and fill it with hot coffee to within one inch of the brim. Add sugar to taste and stir. Top off with whipped cream by pouring it over the back of a spoon on to the drink.

Heavenly!

We Love the Irish but . . .

VISITORS TO IRELAND in the past have not always been flattering. While we can't accept the truth of their statements it would be wrong to ignore what they said.

Around 1190 the bold Giraldus Cambrensis wrote, ". . . immersed in sloth, their greatest delight is to be exempt from toil, their richest possession the enjoyment of liberty . . . This people, then, is truly barbarous, being not only barbarous in their dress but suffering their hair and beards to grow enormously in an uncouth manner, just like the modern fashion recently introduced . . . Whatever natural gifts they possess are excellent, in whatever requires industry they are worthless."

Needless to remark the bold Giraldus was biased and prejudiced.

To be fair, not all Englishmen spoke like that of us and Thomas Gainsford, a soldier of the sixteenth century, wrote, "They have strong and able bodies, proud hearts, pestilent wits, amorous (wherein their women are extraordinarily pleased), patient to endure, lovers of music and hospitality, constant to their maintainers, whether men or women, implacable in their hatred, light of belief, covetous of glory, impatient of insult . . ."

Rural Blarney

If INTERPOL or the United Nations get on the track of the narcotic that is the Blarney of rural Ireland the addiction will be totally banned. The appetite can't be cured or eased; and once it gets a grip the victim will be found wandering the roads of the land and he drinking and making merry with the fine country people until his money or his liver gives out.

It is as warm and slow-moving as a river of honey; as crisply beautiful as a bar of bullion and as fresh in texture and flavour as a newly sliced lemon. Stir that mixture with a heavy addition of exotic and fragrant peat smoke and you have an improbable notion of what the whole thing is like. Wander too far, once you get it in your blood stream, and you'll wake screaming in the night looking for a "fix".

Wherever the stranger goes, from the kindly, honest charms of Co. Donegal to the subtle smooth and nebulous attractions of Co. Cork, he'll be the centre of interest. In Westmeath they'll make him feel like Napoleon and one wave of a sword and they'll answer to his command like the Imperial Guard at Waterloo; in Co. Clare they'll make him feel like a tribal chief with the right to lend his wife to nobles of equal status at any hour of the day or night.

Nothing But Good

Here beyond the cities and the towns you will find the

purest Blarney – the fanatical devotion to a courtesy that insists you must not be worried about anything in the whole wide creation of God. They are not flattering you nor are they servile – and underneath their soothing front is the steel pride of a Spanish hidalgo – but they mean you well.

They'll go to endless lengths to say something good of you and I remember one churl from the suburbs of California who almost distracted a small hotel. When he was gone I tried to coax the proprietor into open condemnation – but no use. All he would agree was: "Ah the man was upsettin' to himself but sure wasn't he very good at it?"

For some strange and unearthly reason many Irish people are ashamed of the "brogue". The city people will blush hotly if you suggest it exists and mutter about stage Irishmen and that sort of thing but it exists and should be preserved.

It is in fact a survival of Elizabethan pronunciation and drop Shakespeare in Co. Mayo and his ears would be more at home than at Oxford. Many Irish country pronunciations are accepted to be the same as those which were used in Elizabethan times.

"Ayther" for "either"; "Nayther" for "neither"; "mate" for "meat"; "sowl" for "soul"; "consayt" for "conceit" – all of these are the English of more than three hundred years ago. Words like "forninst" for instance were used at that time also. (See "Shakespeare Blarney" on page 35).

The Charmers' Charmers

In any event, the lilt and flow of the Irish country accents is absolutely charming, even to ourselves. It is expressive and full of shades and tones that would charm the chromium off a plated teapot.

No matter what you say, they'll try and find a way to comfort and enchant you. Complain about the weather and say, "The rain is awful. I hate the weather here."

You may get the reply I once heard given by a rural

Tallyrand which assuaged the feeling of the complainant while not offering him a flattering optimism.

"Ah, if you don't like the weather here you can always move on a piece and not like the weather there ayther."

If you want to bring joy to rural Ireland, have a long chat with it on the subject of its health. This is very dear to its little heart and it will be delighted to discourse on the subject with enthusiasm.

The Eloquent Bowels

The adult rural population is very much concerned with constipation which the malicious suggest is a substitute for sex – but scorn the begrudgers. The hobby is pursued for its own sake. One does not wish to offend the susceptibilities of delicate-minded readers but the pursuit of truth compels me to say that the Irish peasant is at his most eloquent when he speaks of his "bowel movements". Disguised in a pint of stout I have heard them ramble on for hours on topics like the "nine day wonder" or senna, man's best friend.

"Well, you see on the sixth day I was a bit upset like and I took a dose of my mother's liver medicine with a wee dropeen of sheep scour just to give it a bit of strength. Sure Big Paddy of the Mountain told me that in the great hot summer he was strangled for all time in the big gut only for the sheep scour. Well, howsoever it may have been an encouragement to Big Paddy of the Mountain, it was without any kindness for me."

"It must have gone hard with you, Mickaleen and you to be sufferin' and moanin' with the terrible gripin' pains that does be on a man and he to be strangled in the big gut. And what did you do to save yourself from the stranglin'? Was it that you drank of the well of the Old Wish Man of Muckeeniderdhasala?"

"Oh, but t'was not indeed. On the eleventh day and the cold sweat fallin' to the green grass of Ireland like the first dew of morning . . ."

"Did you hear him say the eleventh day, Sean Mickaleen Thomas . . ."

"I did surely and 'tis a high wonder to the whole parish . . ."

The victim bows and waits for the soft breeze of their sympathy to blow over the gratified surfaces of his ego. There is silence. He resumes.

"On the twelfth day . . ."

"Glory be to the high hills of the McGillicuddy Reeks!"

". . . . I was running on the tarred road hopin' t'would have the power to do me good when I was struck by the morning bus to Galway City."

" 'Tis not the like of this you'd be after hearin' in the fields of New York or the by-roads of Chicago, London, Birmingham or Coventry!"

"... And when it had gone by and I pulled myself from the ditch I found a quare change had come over me and I felt like a boy of eighteen again there was such power in my limbs and free movement in the roped muscles of my body. I'm telling you there's Almighty power in the radiator of a bus to free the strangled gut of a man betimes."

There is a long silence undisturbed by nothing more than the scurry of one or two citizens running to be in time for the 5.30 p.m. service from Clifden to Galway. And this is how it is and don't be after thinking that it is the bothered carelessness of the lightheaded that has the men – yes, and the women too – bounding along with great buck leps over the wide, bright roads of Eireann. 'Tis waiting for buses they are surely.

This may indicate a little of the preoccupation of the people with a vital matter. As I said you can Blarney them from here to the birthplace of Glauber on the subject.

Soft – or Cruel Entirely

Next to health, the weather is perennial Blarney material. There are so many shades of climate that it takes the best part of any day to arrive at an assessment of its condition. Not for the good Irish peasant the complexity of depressions or ridges of high temperature. For him it can be a soft day (two inches of rain) or "a cruel day entirely".

"A cruel day entirely," is one on which the paint is blown off doors and the population is throwing lifebelts to ducks. It is, of course, one of the Irish Blarney illusions that they suffer from bad weather, and a great deal of time in climate discussions goes on analysing "weather" it is this or "weather" it is that.

"Will it be after raining, Poudeen?"

"Well the wind is coming from the back of the mountain and 'tis a bad sign."

"Joe Mary's corn is not sending the hot burning pains of Hell up his left leg he tells me and this is a sign of a dry week."

"That corn itself will be the ruin of the parish betimes. Wasn't it last year that we went out to cut the hay because Joe Mary told us and wasn't it we that had to be taken from the low meadow by boat. Look at the ridge of clouds there over by Shaun Liam the grocer. Isn't there the weight of the Atlantic wrapped in it."

"You have the right of it but man and boy I've believed in Joe Mary's corn and maybe it is the good man that might have the truth of it. 'Tis his corn that is the pride of the five parishes."

The Night of the Big Wind

It is a standard joke in Ireland to introduce the Night of the Big Wind into conversation. It is typical of the Irish that they remember this storm of over a century ago when they can't tell you what was the major political event of the time.

Bear it in mind – health and weather will do much to divert Blarney from your head. On the other hand you will find a dangerous weakening in your power to resist Blarney if you have some complaint or illness which enables rural Ireland to offer you its sympathy.

Inform it of your headache or your digestive upset and it'll spring to soothing, intensively sympathetic action. Rural Ireland will, above all, want to know if your tongue is "coated" and in its diagnostic liturgy there is no greater indication of ill-health.

It will advise you to "clear out your system" and leans heavily towards Glauber Salts and Senna for this purpose. Senna Blarney is something that will really move you.

Do not expect a happy optimism in conversation to give you a psychological uplift; the sympathy they'll give you will be coloured by an almost absolute pessimism which clearly marks you down for something awful with plague in it. You are sitting outside your hotel, feeling recovery in your blood when a native son stops to speak.

"Are you better?"

"I am feeling somewhat better, thank you."

"You do? Well, now I'd say to you to be careful. You have an awful yellow look in the whites of your eyes that my poor cousin Sarah had last winter."

You investigate: "And what effect had that yellow colour

on your cousin Sarah? Was it eventually cured?"

"Don't know . . . and I'm not telling you a word of a lie. She died too soon afterwards for us to be sure if it was unhealthy."

You're Looking Bad . . .

Of course this sort of thing puts you in their power completely. Desperate for one single crumb of comfort from their authoritative and decisive lips you'll do anything to earn it. You'll do even more to avoid their standard greeting in illness.

"How are you feeling . . . you're looking awful bad."

On the other hand if you indicate that you are depressed it will be worse – their synthetic optimism will chill the blood in your veins.

"I wouldn't worry too much about that weakness in the chest. It'll do you no harm. My brother Liam Shaun had it for years – the Lord have mercy on him."

Indeed the sagest advice that can be given on health Blarney in rural Ireland is never to admit to any feeling of ill-health. If you do feel something coming on – get out and fast.

The Ego-Inflaters

But as I've said the purest, best and nicest Blarney is to be found outside urban Ireland. If you want to have your ego gently and smoothly inflated, go on your own into a country public house and involve yourself in the conversation. You'll have a ball. It's the type of conversation you've dreamed about all your life. No one contradicts you; no smart Alec corrects your facts; no one tries to outdo you and the attention of your audience is complete in its devout respect.

"Did you read, Mickleen Pat, of the Russia man's new rocket?"

"I did indeed, Shauneen, and sure aren't they full of brains."

You desire to correct these views.

"Look, I don't want to interrupt . . ."

"Go on and welcome!"

"Sure, we're glad you . . ."

You hesitate but the rapt attention of your audience; their eager anticipation of your words make it easy.

"Look, this is the position about the competition in world armaments . . ."

You go on. They listen, nodding enthusiastically to show how much they appreciate your wisdom. At intervals you'll hear whispered exclamations from the crowd round you.

"Hasn't he the brains of the world!"

"The education is at him, Praise be to the High Saints of Heaven!"

Very gratifying. Very.

The Family Way

Kinships is another important topic in rural Ireland. If you are passing along some boreen and it rains you may be asked to shelter in one of the houses along the way. Shelter will include an invitation to have ". . . a cup of tay in your hand and a bit of seedy cake."

Accept. Rural Ireland is sensitive on the question of its hospitality and you must never reflect on its "seedy" cake by a refusal. Once you accept you take on the obligation to comment on the weather, past, present and future with some observations on its political, historical, geological and psychic influence. When this is over the conversation will drift delicately to yourself.

"You'd be a stranger around here I'd be after thinking?"

Admit it.

"You have the great look about you of the O'Connors of Ballynascubeen. You wouldn't have any relationship with them by any chance?"

Do not deny it absolutely for you would deprive them of the simple Blarney amusements of do-it-yourself genealogy.

"Thomaseen, would he be one of the Black O'Connors from over by the crossroads?"

"Ah, no, mother sure none of thim went to America. 'Tis how he might be a second cousin once removed of Patrick Mary Joseph, the blacksmith."

"Oh, Thomaseen, that couldn't be at all. T'was Patrick Mary Joseph's brother's wife that went to Boston and sure she was one of the Gleesons of Dunridinnamina. Maybe the man is connected by marriage with . . ."

This could go to the edge of the night and if you weren't careful you'd be waterlogged with tea and strangled in the big gut from seedy cake by the time it was over.

Yes – you'll find lots of Blarney in rural Ireland but it is the kind that will warm the cockles of your heart and skin the acids of life's weariness from your soul and thoughts. There's no one like them – God bless them every one.

Tory Island's Revolving Saint

TORY ISLAND is a grim Atlantic outpost in the north-west of Ireland. It was here the Holy children of the King of India are alleged to have come to see St. Columcille. It is told that no sooner did they land on the island than they dropped dead from fatigue.

The saint was summoned and realizing the obligations of Irish hospitality he prayed for their restoration to life. When his prayer was answered he explained to the Indians – six brothers and a sister – that he could only keep them alive long enough to hear their confessions and to give them the last sacraments. They – not to be outdone – accepted his explanation and courteously dropped dead again when the ceremonies were over. All were buried with solemnity.

Unfortunately the girl showed a disconcerting unwillingness to remain buried and nightly her body revolved to the surface no matter how often she was re-buried. St. Columcille solved that one as well.

"It is," he is supposed to have said, "that her virginity is offended by being buried with six men even though they be her brothers."

They re-interred her in puritanical seclusion and she was at peace. The visitor should console himself with this example of the grave courtesy of the Irish and their kindness to the Revolving Saint of Tory Island.

Poetic Blarney

ONCE UPON A TIME Ireland was swarming with poets who wandered the country seeking hospitality and using their verbal skills to damn all who refused them. Their demands were quite unique and it is on record that six hundred of them with their wives and servants and over one hundred hounds descended on the generous King Guaire of Connacht and demanded that he give them enough cuckoos to sing to them between Big and Small Christmas. It could have been the origin of the phrase, "going cuckoo".

United Blarney States

THE CONTRIBUTION of the Irish to the making and the ruling of the United States was out of all proportion to their numbers. Of those who signed the American Declaration of Independence some 15 per cent were Irish. Almost one third of the United States' Presidents have been of Irish origin and these include the great Andrew Jackson, Polk, Buchanan, Andrew Johnson, Grant, Arthur, Cleveland, Harrison, McKinley, Wilson and, of course, John F. Kennedy. To list all of those who gave of their green blood and effort to forge the Union would be impossible but a few names at random may indicate the range of Irish influence. Davy Crockett was Irish and so too were Stephen Foster, Edgar Allan Poe, Sam Houston, Horace Greeley and many others. When, oh, when will they give Ireland back her lost fifty states of America?

Motorised Blarney

OUTSIDE THE CITIES the traffic density in Ireland, even at the height of summer, is very low. Eight cars travelling in a group at sixty miles an hour is an Irish traffic jam. You won't be Blarneying the natives when you tell them they have a vast network of first-class roads. At the same time I am sceptical of the story told by one visitor from London describing how when he drove into a mountain village in Co. Donegal the natives gathered around shouting, "The horseless carriage has come! The horseless carriage has come!"

Automobile Blarney includes an almost total exemption for the tourist from the traffic laws. An English, American, or even a foreign number plate is an open permit to the freedom of the roads. It is only courteous to respond by not knocking down too many of the citizens who might feel hurt at your lack of consideration. Property is another thing and the telegraph poles and the lamp standards of the nation are at your disposal if you want to play Motorized Ten-Pin Bowling, an exhilarating if expensive sport. It is very popular with the locals.

The Green Elephant Test

The drunken driving laws are far more liberal than in other countries and the main – if unofficial – guide to intoxication is the Blarney-Multiple-Green-Elephant-Optical

Test. In simple terms this means that no one is considered incapable until he or she has started to see doubled images of their Green Elephant hallucinations. A fair and just system, it will be realized.

There is the story of the man who was herding his green elephants to his car when he was stopped by a policeman or as we call them a *Garda Siochana na Eireann* (A Guardian of the Peace in Ireland). As he left the public house behind him and rested a moment against the petrol pump (almost all Irish public houses have petrol pumps and it is widely suggested that they are used by the thirstier alcohol seekers) the Guardian of the Peace in Ireland wagged a finger at him.

"Do you tell me now," he said solemnly, "that you're going to drive yourself home in that state . . ."

"Arrah, begob, musha and bejapers," said the drunk, taking full advantage of the Blarney Atmospheric Sonic Warp, "can't you see I'm in no condition to walk?" (See *Best Irish Jokes* (Wolfe Publishing, 5s.) retold by Anthony Butler).

Stunned by the logic of it the Guardian of the Peace in Ireland stood to one side and allowed the herd to be driven past him. Let's be honest – the alien will be given even greater scope.

Bending the Law

So warmly is Blarney applied to the driving visitor that not alone are the human laws bent in his favour but the laws of Nature too are amended where necessary. Another story may illustrate the Stationary-Car-in-Motion-Blarney.

A native was parked in a village street when a tourist swung down the centre of the road in his big American automatic transmission automobile – an immoral thing, surely, with no gear lever to come between man and maid – and smashed into the back of the immobile vehicle. Indignant, the native, sadly overlooking his Blarney duty to the visitor – went for a Guardian of the Peace in Ireland who came and surveyed the damage. The Guardian looked at the blended cars and then came around to the window of the offending driver.

"Look, now, me spalpeen," he growled, "and what is it you think you would be up to entirely, surely, and you to be mating your big car by violent artificial insemination to this poor man's wee vehicle contrary to the Road Traffic Acts of this nation?"

The offending one blushed, shrunk and mumbled apologies.

"Look, Officer, I wanna say I'm mighty, mighty sorry for this . . ."

The accent was plainly that of the next parish, three thousand miles away across the Atlantic.

"Wait now . . . wait now," the Guardian asked with shocked surprise, "Is it a visitor you are itself?"

Then remembering his personal Blarney duty to the Atmospheric Sonic Warp, he added, "Bejapers, Musha, Begob, and indubitably, Arrah."

"Guess, Officer, you could say I'm a visitor to your lovely Island and I admire your policemen . . ."

"Enough . . . enough," grinned the Law, "drive on there and when you've passed over the hill – look to the left as you do to see the Ancient Standing Stones, archaeological remains of great antiquity and interest – I'll have a word with this *amaden* (fool) who backed into you."

This story may not be true, but in Ireland a story that deserves to be true is given full factual status. So it must be taken for real.

Instant Beef

In general, the farmers of Ireland have a very high respect for those who come amongst us but they don't see anything wrong with driving herds of cows or bullocks on to fast motorways – and sure isn't there more room on those?

This may not Blarney the tourist but some say it accounts for the large quantity of beef produced in this country. It can save butchering costs to drive the cattle on to the roads.

You can turn around a corner and find yourself in the middle of such a herd and you have to swing this way and that to avoid the curiosity of the things. The farmer will cycle up beside you – always glad to make easy and pleasant the way of the stranger. With the noise of the cattle and your engine he can't hear much of what you say but he's on your side in any case.

"Get those cattle to hell out of it."

He nods amiably.

"The weather is good rightly and t'will stay settled I'll be after thinking. Have ye come far?"

"Will you clear a blanketty-blank path for me?"

He laughs heartily. "You have a fine way of telling it but 'tis the fine free roads we have here as you say. You can drive for miles and not meet one car forninst ye."

Some textbooks recommend that the visitor climb out and gently strangle the farmer with his own bicycle but in my view nothing can justify this. It could delay you for half an hour if you tried to do the job properly. It is simpler to let in the clutch and put your foot down. There is hardly anything lovelier in the late evening light than to see the golden slanting rays of the sun across the backs of cattle as they clear hedges and fences for several miles around with quick easy grace.

You have little hope with sheep as they have no chaperon or "sheeperon" as I assume they should be called. Compared with Irish black-faced sheep, the average native bullock is crippled in all four legs and it would warm the heart of John Peel to see them skim the countryside when a tourist cuts a mutton-productive swathe amongst them. On the other hand you can have good fun trying to race mountain sheep and you can sometimes keep up with them for half an hour if they happen to be tired when starting.

A very large number of sheep are annually transformed into instant-knitting by the simple bang of a chromium-plated radiator. Knit yourself one.

Lost? Ask a Peasant

At some stage in your wandering around Ireland, you are bound to get lost in one of the remoter areas. It happens to all of us. You can use a map to find your way back to an identifiable town, village or road; alternatively you can ask a passing peasant.

Maps are, of course, highly technical, and in order to use them you have to know where you are, while if you know where you are you don't need a map. It could be that as you look around unfamiliar territory in Darkest Ireland you may *have* to rely on a passing peasant – if and when he passes.

They are rare and shy and prefer to lurk rather than pass. Unknown to you there may be hordes of them diverting across the fields to avoid you. They have been asked questions before.

Eventually you may lay hands on one by digging holes in the road and covering them with straw. Try and recover your specimen in undamaged condition if you can.

Let us assume you have one rural dweller near you and you open the palaver with a courteous greeting.

"Good afternoon," you say sweetly and then add, in the manner of the country, "The blessing of St. Monica and the Holy Virgins of Nurnberg be on you."

You may touch a chord in his bosom and if so he will respond warmly.

"The blessing of St. Monica and the Holy Virgins of Nurnberg no less than that of St. Patrick, St. Brigid, St. Brendan and St. Fechin be upon you too."

You need his help so don't stint the preliminaries and continue, "The blessing of St. Monica and the Holy Virgins of Nurnberg, St. Patrick, St. Brigid, St. Brendan, St. Fechin, St. Anthony, St. Paul, St. Peter and Saints Damien and Cosmos be on you in addition."

He will take a deep breath, step back a mental pace or two and run at it: "The blessing of St. Monica and the Holy Virgins of Nurnberg, St. Patrick – and could I do anything for ye?"

A good sign. He's breaking down and you are one up.

"Could you tell me if we are far from Ballynascubeen?"

Where You're Not

He broods and draws prophetic patterns in the dust with his foot. You wait and know it will be good when it comes. He raises his head and you activate your ear drums.

"No, then," he'll hint shrewdly, "I can tell you you're not."

As he shrinks back into a contemplative trance once more you work out the next part of the dialogue. You find what you imagine is the perfect and most lucid query to stymie any evasion or ambiguity.

"What way should we go then?"

"That way," he answers with a wave of his hand that

takes in all the points of the compass and about five-sixths of the immediate landscape.

Your wife, girl-friend or companion may become irate at this and savagely urge you to offer beads or a trading knife. Do not heed such advice and remember you are at this man's mercy and in any case he didn't compel you to bother him as he strolled by. Work out another section of the script.

"Thank you, but could you tell me which road to take?"

He sinks into a trance once more and having communed with his inner being surfaces long enough to say, "Take the straight road and you can't miss it."

It is not a very consistent statement for both behind and in front the "straight" road twists like a corkscrew in search of whiskey. Nothing further is to be gained by questioning. You have squeezed him of information to the pulp of his being and you press on. Many passing peasants are highly intelligent – in fact most of them are – but they are too intelligent to pass anyone who is lost.

The Eager Youth

You may think you will have better luck with the young generation and you are aware of the advances being made in education. Observe passing children until you find one with a large expanse of forehead or some other sign of high I.Q.

"Sonny, could you direct me to Ballynascubeen?"

He is eagerness itself.

"Yes, sir, I can, sir. I'll tell you, sir. Do you know my uncle's house down the road, sir?"

"I do not know your uncle's house down the road. In fact I do not know your uncle."

"His name is Billy Maher, sir."

Breathing hard and restraining yourself from speaking harshly of his uncle you again ask for directions.

"Well, sir, do you know the house down at the cross-roads that was burnt last year?"

You pass on.

Petrol and a Quick One

In the end you will probably have to decide to buy more petrol and although there may not be crocks of gold at the end of all Irish rainbows there's a public house at the end of almost all petrol pumps in rural Ireland. What better could you do than decide to go in, have a quick one and work out your location with the kindly proprietor?

You leave your car in the hands of the youth who acts as servant of the pump and enter.

Inside you will find out why there is a scarcity of passing peasants. Seated on stools and chairs is a high proportion of the local population consoling each other that they can't work because it is too wet or too dry. They are tackling large glasses of liquid alcohol like engineers sinking artesian wells.

Heads raise at your coming. Silence falls.

You order a glass of Irish whiskey as a preliminary to finding out where you are and in due time the barman will bring it and cryptically announce, "Soft day. Is it travelling you are?"

A splendid opening and you take advantage of it, "Yes, I am. As a matter of fact, I'm looking for Ballynascubeen."

It is a Blarney rule in the Irish public house that the proprietor answers no questions himself. He passes the query on to the customers like a referee throwing in the ball.

Follow the Signposts

"Mick, what's the best way to Ballynascubeen?"

The chorus is deafening. Mick, Patrick, John, Joseph, Willie, Shaun and Pascal Xavier Emmanuel offer their collective advice . . .

"Go down to the turnpike . . ."

"Better to take the shortcut across the quarry road . . ."

"Go back the way you came . . ."

"Go straight on . . ."

"Follow the signposts . . ."

In the controversy that will rage you may have time to consider what is a standard direction in Ireland. "Follow the signposts." One pictures them as highly mobile – racing along the roads followed by happy tourists and leading them carefully to where ever they wish to go. Be prepared, however, for you will be told again and again to follow them.

After the initial excitement the conference will settle down into a more orderly discussion.

"If he was to be after goin' and takin' the first blessed turn to the right after the half-crossroads itself . . ."

"Cassidy, 'tis not the first turn to the right . . ."

" 'Tis unless you would be after counting Micky Joe's boreen (little road) or is it that you do be thinking of?"

Another moves in.

" 'Twould be too difficult surely for them that does not be knowin' the lay of the land. Let him be after going on to the Big Tree four miles forninst him and then taking the big arm of the three-forked road past the mill and not the one after Rafferty the seed merchant he'd . . ."

The meeting will not reach agreement and there will be argument and counter-argument. In the meantime you will consider it the merest courtesy to refresh your advisers and the whole thing takes on a social tinge. Eventually it is wise to tear yourself away assuring all of them that you will follow the signposts. They wave you on your way with enthusiasm asking no more of you but that you tell their first cousin once removed in Birmingham, Coventry, New York, Chicago, Honolulu, Hong Kong or Samoa that they were asking for them.

You might as well go through all this but in the end use the map. That way you can lose yourself without assistance.

Blarney at the Pumps

It might be no harm to warn about the Blarney of petrol pump attendants. They are insidious and to fall for their conversation is fatal.

All of these young men have ambition – they would be farm labourers if they hadn't – and they see every English or American tourist and some foreign visitors as potential fairy Godmothers who will offer them magnificent jobs abroad in vast palatial filling stations.

No matter what your inclination confine yourself to monosyllables as they butter you with Blarney like a piece of French toast.

" 'Tis a fine car you have, sir?" They look at you keenly assessing how many petrol stations you own.

"Yes," you say, coldly and brutally.

"This year's model?"

"Yes."

"I like this model the best of all. I think anyone with a bit of regard for motors would pick it. Would you think so yourself?"

"Yes."

"Are you getting much to the gallon, sir?"

This is a difficult question which is intended to tempt you from the straight and narrow but do not be tempted. Answer with a simple and emphatic, "Yes".

"Will I check at the tyre pressures, sir?"

"Yes."

"What pressures do you like, sir?"

Once more you are faced with a dilemma but depending on the type of attendant it is safer to stick to the script and answer "Yes".

Undoubtedly you will go on your way with 42 pounds in the rear right; 28 in the left front; 12 in the rear left, and a soaring 72 in the front right. When you get used to it you will be surprised how infrequently you'll feel seasick.

Deviation from the suggested script, however, can be

fatal and due to careless talk one Birmingham tourist found himself host to seventeen Irish attendants looking for jobs as British petrol pump attendants.

These then are some of the hazards and pleasures of Blarney driving in Ireland and remember that at the end of each season all unclaimed tourists are collected and given good homes as far as possible. So don't fear the worst – it could be much better than you imagined.

Poteen

POTEEN is an illegal brew which is distilled largely in the west of Ireland where a continuous game of hide and seek is played by the police and the illicit distillers. It is quite expensive, due to the glamour that attaches to its production but generally speaking it is a wretched and often dangerous concoction. It is made from all kinds of ingredients including pig-meal, treacle, sawdust and almost anything the makers can lay hands on. To give it body, the stuff is sometimes blended with sulphuric acid, carbide and soap.

Drisheen

No MENTION of Blarney would be complete without a mention of Drisheen which is a famous Co. Cork delicacy. Kissing the Blarney Stone may give eloquence but no one knows what eating Drisheen gives and the most the non-Corkonian can hope is that it is curable.

It must be remembered that the inhabitants of Co. Cork are different to the rest of their fellow countrymen. Ambitious, intelligent, efficient and very hard working, they are in some ways the Prussians of Ireland. They provide Ireland with many of its civil servants, its policemen and its business executives.

The secret of Co. Cork's greatness may lie in Drisheen and the following recipe will help you to produce a reasonable facsimile of the stuff.

First you'll require a quart of fresh sheep's blood and the moment you get it dash home where the little woman should be waiting with a quart of milk and a quart of cream; one pint of fine white bread crumbs; four ounces of finely chopped mutton suet; one dessertspoon of salt; a half level teaspoon of white pepper; a half level teaspoon of fresh thyme leaves; some fresh scalded sage and a small pinch of tansey and also mace.

The herbs are crumbled and rubbed through a sieve with a pinch of mace. As soon as the blood arrives it is mixed with the salt and when it is thoroughly blended the whole thing is strained through a piece of muslin or fine cloth.

The milk, pepper and the crumbled herbs are mixed and heated slightly to something not above tepid. This too is strained and added to the blood. After five minutes mixing, the suet and breadcrumbs are added.

The ideal thing is to stow the whole mixture in the intestines of a pig – a dead one we must insist. If pig intestines are not available the stuff is spread about three inches in depth in a large tin or casserole which will fit into a saucepan. The saucepan is filled with warm water up to an inch below the level of the Drisheen. Covered with grease-proof paper it is cooked in a moderate oven – Regulo 2 or 200 degrees F. – for forty minutes. Cooled, it is cut into fingers and grilled or baked for about seven minutes in a hot oven. It is served with sausages, bacon, tomatoes, etc.

So there you are – you too can make Drisheen but we wonder. There probably is some secret ingredient which they keep secret or some Druidic incantation that's been handed down for centuries. In any event, make it if you can – and eat it if you dare.

Blarney Borrowing

THE THOUGHT of finding yourself short of money in Ireland might bring you from the sound, decent sleep of the night with loud lamentations and a tearing of the sweet locks of your head. You can be certain – and may St. Frigidien and St. Sigisbert be witness – that the like will not be troubling you through the length and breadth of the fair land.

No Irishman would refuse to lend you money and his only worry would be that you might shame him by bringing your request to someone else.

"And sure is that all you would be this day asking forninst me? 'Tis a sum that I would not toss to a tinker without doublin' and treblin' it to the last halfpenny. Spake your mind, let ye, and nather stint nor bind nor diminish your need. So long as I have it you can suckle your fill at the whole of my store without let, leave or command."

Making due allowance for Blarney Atmospheric Sonic Warp the message will come through loud and clear and total. It will end with a suggestion that the business be wrapped up with a drink, lunch or a dinner.

"Splendid," you say to yourself, and likewise, "excellent."

What Price Reality?

You will admire the tact, the generosity, the diplomacy, the humanity of the response but it has one snag. The

appearance of the loan in actual hard cash is slow to materialize. It could be that the Irish are unwilling to spoil a magnanimous act by introducing sordid actualities, or else they feel that the agreement to lend is enough in itself. Whatever the reason, there is a wide gap between the warm assurance and the cold reality.

On the other hand you will find that money is not always essential and a good, open, honest, cheerful, kindly face is as good as a credit card.

Indeed the Irish almost created a new economic system based on the good, open, honest, cheerful kindly face when all the banks closed one time for a long and beautiful strike. The old saying, "His face was his fortune" was literally true.

The economy boomed. Weary publicans had to employ masseurs to keep their bottle opening arms in action. "Instant" money was the order of the day and cheques circulated with a thousand endorsements until they looked like autograph albums. Then the strike ended and almost crippled the country. Money, it was said bitterly on all sides, is only an obstacle to financial progress.

You may find it hard to Blarney actual money out of an Irishman, but he'll hand you an introduction to all who can give you credit. And what more do you want? You'll have to be fairly tough with those you deal with. After all, it's not as if you were giving them cash.

Nothing but the Best

A bold and sweeping approach is best and a niggardly penny-pinching purchasing policy will only destroy confidence in your ability to pay. On credit you must not only order the best – you must order lots of it. The average Irish businessman will assess your financial status on the amount and quality of what you need.

If you use money it is possible to get away with ordering one dozen bottles of Guinness but in Ireland if the shopkeeper gives you credit he'll expect you to demand champagne.

A classical example of this occurred in Ballinasloe, Co. Galway where a bold individual took over a local castle for three months on approval – rent payable at the end of that time. His vast orders were fought over by local shopkeepers and he obtained thousands of pounds worth of credit before it became apparent that he hadn't a penny.

It is not suggested that the visitor practising Blarney credit should be dishonest but he might as well realize that it has obligations that can't be ignored.

One source of money is the Irish Government which is always ready to help the stranger as long as he can indicate that he is doing something to establish a new industry. All you have to do is to pop along and see a Senior Civil Servant. The Blarney Atmospheric Sonic Warp tends, in his case, to operate in triplicate which accounts for some of the peculiar effects you get.

The Magic Words

Utter the phrase "New Industry" to him and you will find that Aladdin's formula "Open Sesame" is scientifically outdated. No sooner have you whispered the words in the ear of the Senior Civil Servant than he bubbles, "Bedad, bedad, bedad," and starts to search the drawers of his desk for bullion bars and ducats of silver. These he will press on you with apologies if his stock is low.

You put down your bullion at your feet and enter into serious negotiation.

"Could I have a loan of a hundred thousand pounds or something like that," you'll mutter and add, "New Industry."

"My dear sir," he'll gasp with shock, "we couldn't possibly – musha, musha, musha – consider loans. If we give you money we must have a binding Blarney contract that in no circumstances will you attempt to repay any part of it. You know – yerra, yerra, yerra – that any other procedure would make you totally ineligible."

He stares at you anxiously.

"If we start making exceptions – Your Honour, sir, Your Honour, sir. Your Honour, sir – everyone else would be looking for the same privilege and we couldn't have that."

To conciliate you, he pulls six antique Georgian silver teapots from his filing cabinet and silently presses them into your pocket. He settles back at his desk.

"I don't want to complain," he'll go on, "but the amount you want – £100,000 – is a bit lower than we normally like to consider from outsiders. You couldn't – musha, musha, musha – make it a million? Just for appearance sake and it's a nice round sum."

There is such pain and anxiety in his eyes you won't be able to resist; with total generosity you'll agree. The hospitality of the Irish imposes obligations.

Before you leave he'll give you the keys to a fully equipped factory, a note to the Tax people not to be bothering you with demands and a free offer of training for your staff.

This is probably the easiest and quickest way of Blarneying cash although you get so much of it that it tends to clutter up the home – a fact which doesn't make it popular with tidy wives. Sometimes the Senior Civil Servant will accept shares or that sort of thing as a souvenir but don't try and pay dividends. He is sensitive.

Anti-Lending Blarney

It might be no harm at this point to tell you the technique of How-Not-to-Lend-Money-to-the-Irish-Blarney. In general you won't be troubled much – we have other ways of tapping the contents of your wallet – but when one of our native "touchers" does try to put the bite on you, study the skill, finesse and sheer talent he'll bring to bear.

The Irish "toucher" is one of the world's greatest actors and there is a strong movement in the country to make him pay entertainment taxes. He'll shrivel your soul with his description of the horrifying disasters that will happen to him if you fail to assist. He'll retreat upstage; clutch his forehead and declaim on your great generosity which alone made it possible for him to ask – something he has never done in his life before. Wife, family and home have unswerving faith in you and when he was leaving the house wasn't the wife dashing off to the butcher to buy their first meal in weeks because she knew you wouldn't let him down.

In other circumstances he will tell you of the fortune you both can make if only you lend him a tenner until Friday. Again he may come and say he's borrowing to help a friend of his. He'll bring tears to your eyes as he describes how he has had to sacrifice his pride to help another.

"If t'were myself now 'tis how I would rather fall down stone, cold and eternally dead than come to ye and ask for money. Poor Paddy now – for him I'd swallow my pride to the last drop to help." You will also find that he'll swallow the last drop of anything else that happens to be around.

He brings perhaps a little too much passion to his task and it is always embarrassing in mixed company to have someone beating their head off the floor with grief – a favourite act of our "touchers" whose heads have worn out more carpets than their shoes.

Sympathise, Sympathise

Difficult though it may be to refuse and disappointing though it may be to miss an Oscar-size performance, only early action can divert him. There are various anti-Borrowing Blarney methods which too can be made to work.

One approach is to let him start off and, judging the time with care, interrupt with a tremendous gush of verbal sympathy. This must take place before he has reached the point of asking – none of them go to the heart of the matter in a hurry.

The moment you have him focused on your words of concern, switch in with the suggestion that he should try and borrow a few pounds from someone. Urge him to forget his pride and to remember his wife and family. Swiftly handled this will leave him speechless long enough for you to streak for the horizon and solvency.

The Blarney-Forward-Financial-Fall is also effective. With this you solve his problem by pointing out it is actually an asset.

If he complains that the landlord is going to evict him point out how fortunate he is to get out of the hands of such a Shylock and express the view that anyone who helped him with money to stay in the clutches of such a man would be no friend. Asserting that you know he would never ask, you still feel bound to say that even if he did you would have to refuse for his own good.

If money is needed to pay a doctor to treat some aged relative or another member of the "toucher's" family protest that it is next to useless to summon medical aid in such a case. Tell him that he must try the remedy you possess. Make it up on the spur of the moment and include spiders' webs, dried seaweed, crushed eggshells and potato water in your prescription – they must cure something.

All of these suggestions are tried and proved. Don't try to evade the issue by fainting or collapsing. On the one occasion we know of it being employed the "toucher" searched his victim before he could fall and dashed off with the announced intention of buying vast quantities of restoratives and stimulants.

The Tinker's Tribute

Perhaps the most elegant in verbal style in their efforts to obtain money are the Irish tinkers. One couldn't say they beg – they levy tribute with almost Shakespearean eloquence.

"The Blessing of God on you, sir, this night and could you help me with the price of a bit of bread? Buy the blessing and prayer of the poor and suffering with a few pence for they have been blown and sluiced by the long winds of the country and the harsh, cruel bite of the frost in the grip of the winter dark . . . etc."

Modest in his demands, the tinker should never be sent on his way with an empty hand. It brings warts on the palm to ignore them.

Auxetophone

IT IS TRUE that the first practical submarine was designed by an Irishman J. P. Holland but we don't get enough credit for the development of the amplification of stringed instruments. Long before electronics took over an inventor Charles Parsons (1854–1927) developed the Auxetophone which was a pneumatic device.

Blarney Farewell

AND EVERYWHERE *there is the magic of Ireland. It smiles with summer racing up the green hill-winds; it plays with white-shaped clouds over the gentle, soft brooding of the reed-bordered lakes; it calls in the long cry of a bird across the great harvest of dusk on the quiet brown of the peat bogs.*

It is the endless cradle of the sea rocking the island with its crooning lilt; it is the sweep of lonely, sun-levelled beaches and it is the far islands that always beckon on the horizon with their undefined promise. It is the sudden fall of valleys on the edge of mountains; it is the polished gloss of roads after rain; it is the fragrance-drenched fields of June and it is the caress of fur-dark rain at the heart of winter; it is music somewhere, nowhere, beyond the horizon, in the sky and all about you.

It is the voice of gentleness and courtesy; it is kindness and laughter and concern; it is the last rooting of the virtues beyond the material and the real. It is bravery and character poured into a mould that is five thousand years old.

Call it what you will – call it Blarney if you like or if you would not seek to shape it in words be content to let it be. A last blessing to you – may the road always rise before you and may God bless and hold you forever in the warm palm of his hand.